moda All-Stars

Snuggle Up!

12 COZY NAP AND LAP QUILTS

Compiled by Lissa Alexander

Martingale
Create with Confidence

Moda All-Stars: Snuggle Up! 12 Cozy Nap and Lap Quilts
© 2022 by Martingale & Company®

Martingale®
18939 120th Ave. NE, Ste. 101
Bothell, WA 98011-9511 USA
ShopMartingale.com

No part of this product may be reproduced in any form, unless otherwise stated, in which case reproduction is limited to the use of the purchaser. The written instructions, photographs, designs, projects, and patterns are intended for the personal, noncommercial use of the retail purchaser and are under federal copyright laws; they are not to be reproduced by any electronic, mechanical, or other means, including informational storage or retrieval systems, for commercial use. Permission is granted to photocopy patterns for the personal use of the retail purchaser. Attention teachers: Martingale encourages you to use this book for teaching, subject to the restrictions stated above.

The information in this book is presented in good faith, but no warranty is given nor results guaranteed. Since Martingale has no control over choice of materials or procedures, the company assumes no responsibility for the use of this information.

Printed in Hong Kong
27 26 25 24 23 22   8 7 6 5 4 3 2 1

Library of Congress Cataloging-in-Publication Data is available upon request.

ISBN: 978-1-68356-177-4

MISSION STATEMENT

We empower makers who use fabric and yarn to make life more enjoyable.

CREDITS

PUBLISHER AND CHIEF VISIONARY OFFICER
Jennifer Erbe Keltner

CONTENT DIRECTOR
Karen Costello Soltys

DESIGN MANAGER
Adrienne Smitke

TECHNICAL EDITOR
Nancy Mahoney

PRODUCTION MANAGER
Regina Girard

COPY EDITOR
Durby Peterson

BOOK DESIGNER
Angie Haupert Hoogensen

ILLUSTRATOR
Sandy Loi

PHOTOGRAPHERS
Adam Albright
Brent Kane

What's your creative passion?
Find it at **ShopMartingale.com**
books • eBooks • ePatterns • blog • free projects
videos • tutorials • inspiration • giveaways

contents

INTRODUCTION 5

projects

CARDINAL CROSSING *by Lynne Boster Hagmeier* 7
FEELING LEAFY *by Corey Yoder* 13
ROLLING PINS *by Barbara Groves and Mary Jacobson* 19
BOARDWALK *by Betsy Chutchian* 25
SPRIGHTLY *by Linzee Kull McCray* 29
GOOD FENCES, GOOD NEIGHBORS *by Robin Pickens* 37
AMERICANA TILES *by Susan Ache* 43
CORAL GARDEN *by Sherri L. McConnell* 49
WOVEN TOGETHER *by Brenda Riddle* 55
SUMMER PICNIC *by Anne Sutton* 61
RUSTIC RETREAT *by Lisa Bongean* 67
PAPER PLANES *by Brigitte Heitland* 75

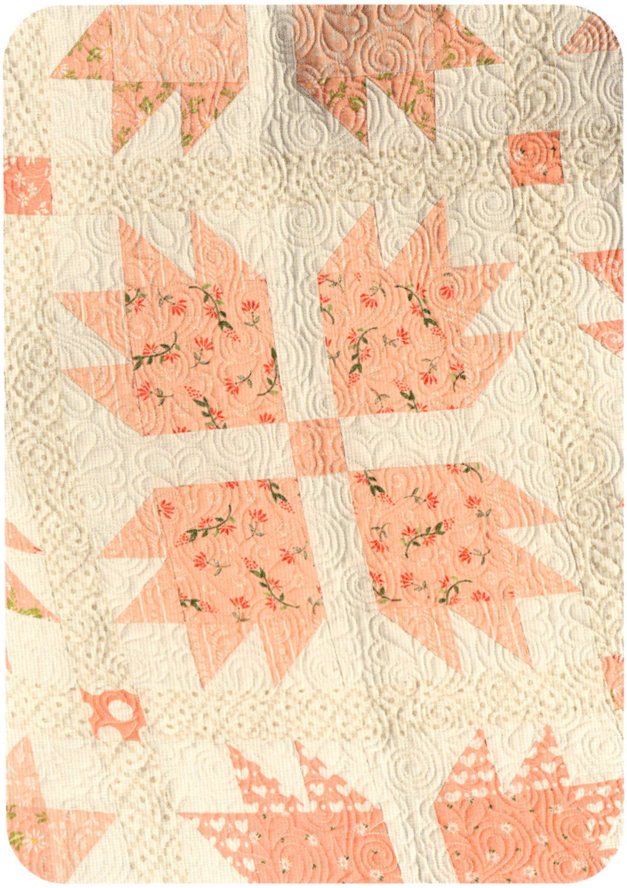
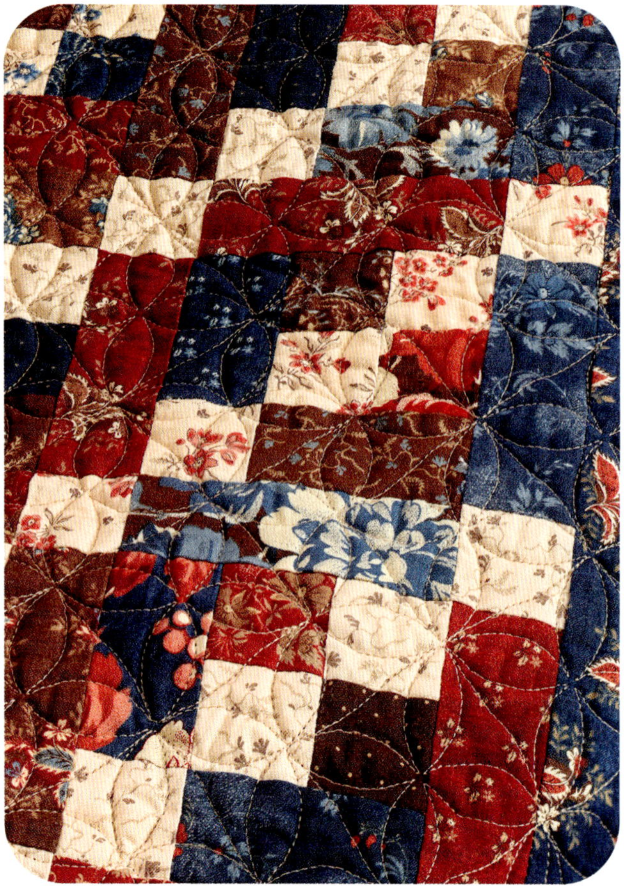
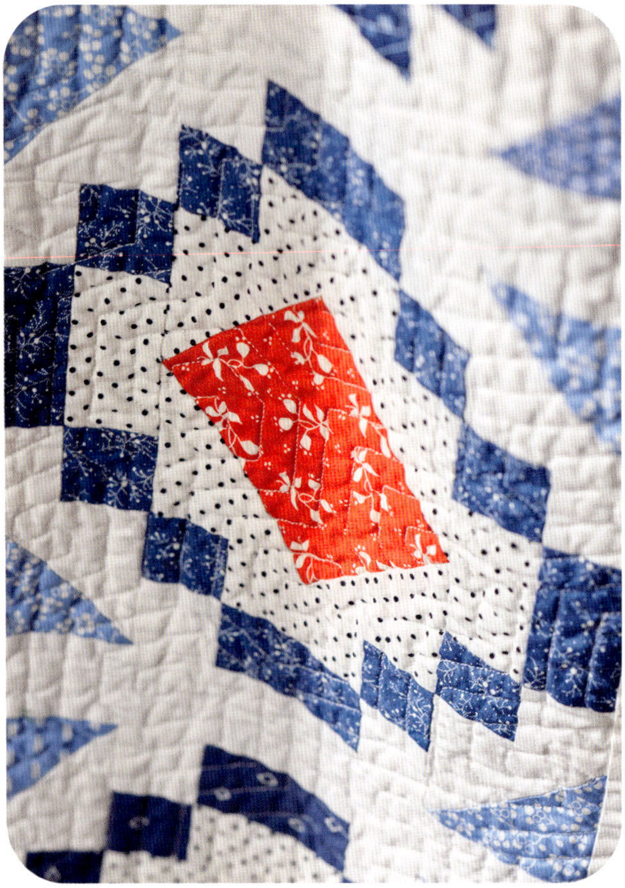
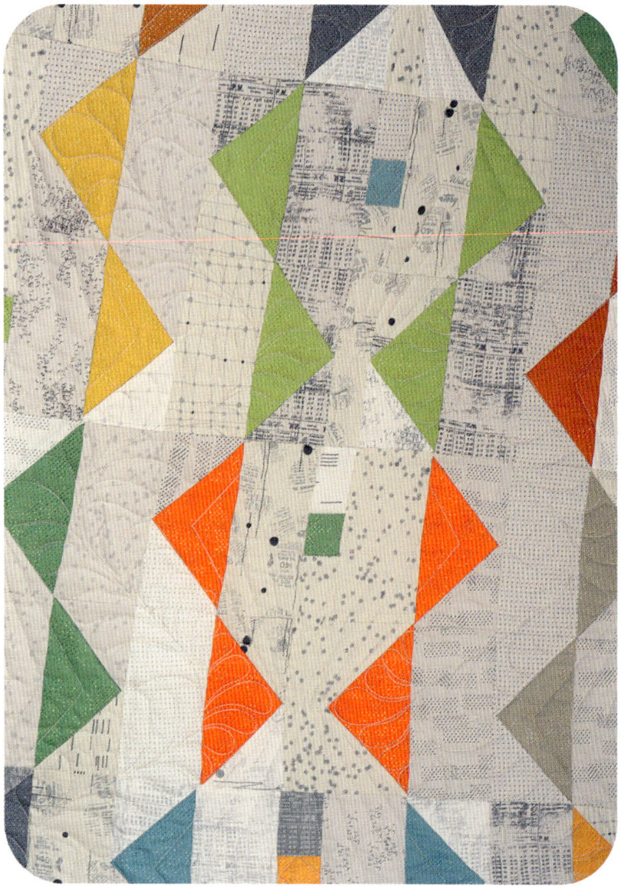

introduction

Relax. Make yourself comfy. Take a little nap. We've got you covered!

How delightful it is to snuggle under a gorgeous lap quilt as you drift off to dreamland. Whether you want to snooze for a while, read a book, watch TV, or just gaze out the window in a moment of quilty bliss, in these pages you'll find lovely patterns for lap quilts to keep you cozy.

Designed by a group of Moda All-Stars, those incredible folks who create fabric lines for Moda, each quilt is a treasure. Let's start with the fabrics. They're fabulous, as you would expect. Inspiring photos invite you to play with plaids and prints, stripes and solids, florals, dots, and more. And the quilt designs are just as enticing. Featuring a variety of styles and color palettes, the projects range from 41" × 51" to 65" × 85" and are relatively quick to finish.

When not in use for snuggling, these quilts are designed to bring joy in other ways as well. You can drape them over the back of a sofa, roll them up in a large basket, or display them on a wall. They're just the right size for taking along in the car, and they make wonderful gifts to warm someone's heart.

Speaking of warming hearts, we're donating the royalties from this book to a worthy cause, just as we've done with every book in the Moda All-Stars series. Your purchase will benefit St. Jude Children's Research Hospital, a charitable organization that provides advanced cures and means of prevention for pediatric catastrophic diseases through research and treatment. Consistent with the vision of its founder, Danny Thomas, no child is denied treatment based on race, religion, or a family's ability to pay.

Wrapping yourself in a lap quilt is like getting a quilted hug. So choose a fun pattern, find some great fabrics, and let's go sew!

—*Lissa Alexander*

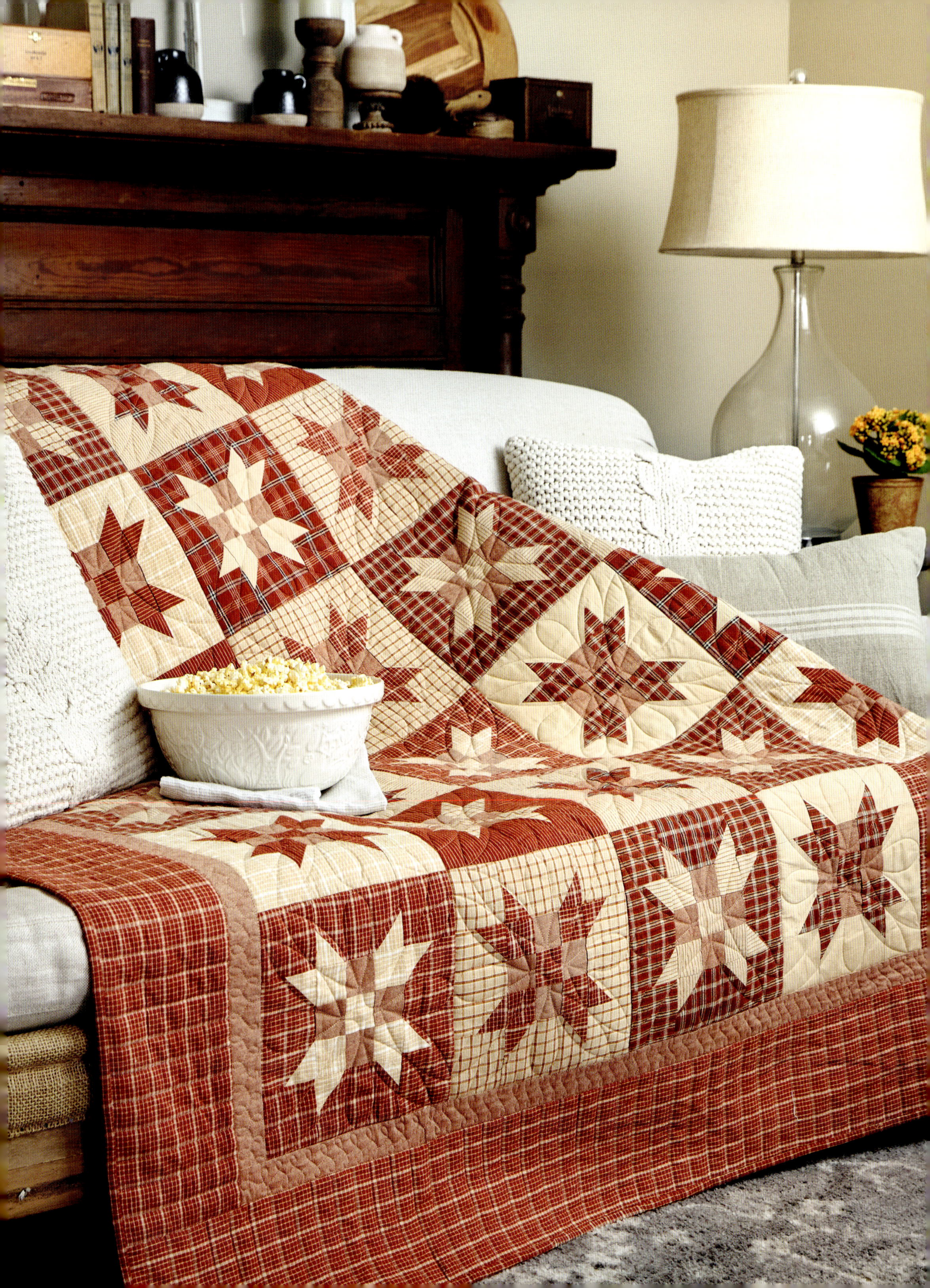

cardinal crossing

On cold winter days in Kansas, Lynne Hagmeier loves to see the bright red cardinals flitting from one branch to another. These crested songbirds are so fun to watch as they hunt for berries. Did you know that only the males are red and the females are a warm caramelly brown? Lynne has put both of those colors to beautiful use in this quilt design.

Designed by Lynne Boster Hagmeier; pieced and quilted by Joy Johnson

materials

Yardage is based on 42"-wide fabric. Lynne used Homemade Homespuns by Kansas Troubles Quilters for Moda Fabrics.

1 yard of light red tone on tone for blocks and inner border

¾ yard *each* of 4 assorted tan plaids for blocks

¾ yard *each* of 3 assorted red A plaids for blocks

3 yards of red B plaid for blocks, outer border, and binding

5¼ yards of fabric for backing

74" × 94" piece of batting

cutting

All measurements include ¼" seam allowances. Keep like pieces together.

From the red tone on tone, cut:
- 16 strips, 2" × 42"; crosscut *9 of the strips* into 35 strips, 2" × 9"

From *each of 2* tan plaids, cut:
- 4 strips, 3¼" × 42"; crosscut into:
    16 pieces, 3¼" × 5" (32 total)
    16 squares, 3¼" × 3¼" (32 total)
- 3 strips, 2" × 42"; crosscut into:
    4 strips, 2" × 9" (8 total)
    36 squares, 2" × 2" (72 total)

From *each of the remaining 2* tan plaids, cut:
- 5 strips, 3¼" × 42"; crosscut into:
    20 pieces, 3¼" × 5" (40 total; 4 are extra)
    20 squares, 3¼" × 3¼" (40 total; 4 are extra)
- 4 strips, 2" × 42"; crosscut into:
    5 strips, 2" × 9" (10 total)
    45 squares, 2" × 2" (90 total)

From *each of 2* red A plaids, cut:
- 4 strips, 3¼" × 42"; crosscut into:
    16 pieces, 3¼" × 5" (32 total)
    16 squares, 3¼" × 3¼" (32 total)
- 3 strips, 2" × 42"; crosscut into:
    4 strips, 2" × 9" (8 total)
    36 squares, 2" × 2" (72 total)

Continued on page 9

FINISHED QUILT:
65½" × 85½"

FINISHED BLOCK:
10" × 10"

8 ♥ *snuggle up!*

Continued from page 7

From the remaining red A plaid, cut:
- 5 strips, 3¼" × 42"; crosscut into:
    - 20 pieces, 3¼" × 5"
    - 20 squares, 3¼" × 3¼"
- 4 strips, 2" × 42"; crosscut into:
    - 5 strips, 2" × 9"
    - 45 squares, 2" × 2"

From the red B plaid, cut on the *crosswise* grain:
- 5 strips, 3¼" × 42"; crosscut into:
    - 20 pieces, 3¼" × 5"
    - 20 squares, 3¼" × 3¼"
- 3 strips, 2" × 42"; crosscut into:
    - 4 strips, 2" × 9"
    - 36 squares, 2" × 2"

From the red B plaid, cut on the *lengthwise* grain:
- 2 strips, 6½" × 73½"
- 2 strips, 6½" × 65½"
- 5 strips, 2½" × 65"

making the tan star blocks

Directions are for making one block. Repeat to make a total of 18 blocks. Press seam allowances in the directions indicated by the arrows. For each block, you'll need the following pieces:

Light red tone on tone: one 2" × 9" strip

Tan plaid: one 2" × 9" strip and nine 2" squares, all matching

Red plaid A or B: four 3¼" × 5" pieces and four 3¼" squares, all matching

1 Join the light red tone-on-tone and tan 2" × 9" strips to make a strip set measuring 3½" × 9", including seam allowances. Cut the strip set into four segments, 2" × 3½".

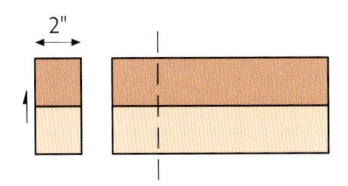

Make 1 strip set, 3½" × 9".
Cut 4 segments, 2" × 3½".

2 Lay out the four segments from step 1 and one tan square as shown. Join the pieces to make a nine-patch unit measuring 5" square, including seam allowances.

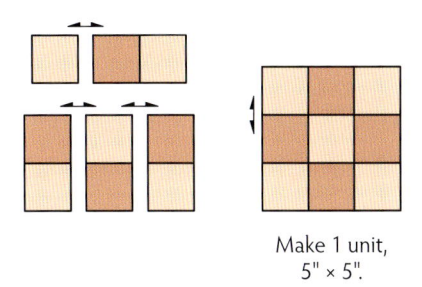

Make 1 unit, 5" × 5".

3 Draw a diagonal line from corner to corner on the wrong side of the remaining tan squares. Place a marked square on one corner of a red piece, right sides together. Sew on the marked line. Trim the excess corner fabric ¼" from the stitched line. Place a marked square on the adjacent corner of the red piece. Sew and trim as before to make a side unit measuring 3¼" × 5", including seam allowances. Make four side units.

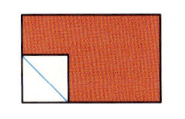

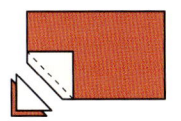

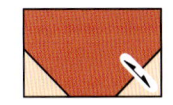

Make 4 units, 3¼" × 5".

TESTING, TESTING

To make sure your folded corners in step 3 are accurate, before trimming, fold open the tan piece along the stitching line to make sure all the edges align. If the top tan triangle doesn't quite meet the edges of the unit, adjust your sewing line by one or two thread widths so the edges of all layers align.

cardinal crossing

4 Lay out four red squares, the four side units, and the nine-patch unit in three rows. Sew the squares and units into rows. Join the rows to make a tan Star block measuring 10½" square, including seam allowances. Repeat the steps to make 18 blocks.

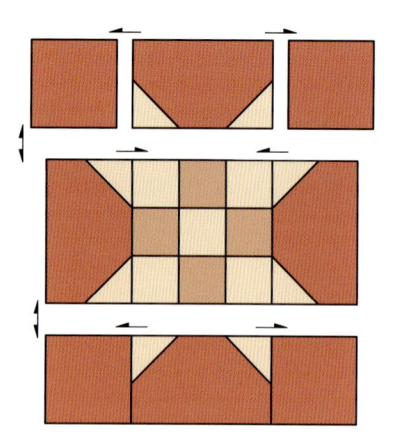

Make 18 tan Star blocks, 10½" × 10½".

making the red star blocks

For each block, you'll need the following pieces. Directions are for making one block. Repeat to make a total of 17 blocks.

Light red tone on tone: one 2" × 9" strip

Red plaid A or B: one 2" × 9" strip and nine 2" squares, all matching

Tan plaid: four 3¼" × 5" pieces and four 3¼" squares, all matching

1 Join the red tone-on-tone and red A or B 2" × 9" strips to make a strip set measuring 3½" × 9", including seam allowances. Cut the strip set into four segments, 2" × 3½".

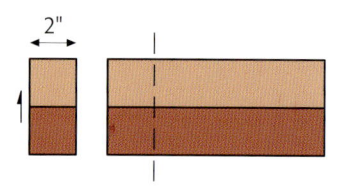

Make 1 strip set, 3½" × 9". Cut 4 segments, 2" × 3½".

10 ♥ snuggle up!

2 Lay out the four segments from step 1 and one red A or B square as shown. Join the pieces to make a nine-patch unit measuring 5" square, including seam allowances.

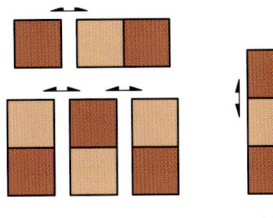

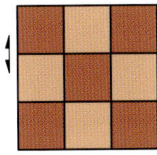

Make 1 unit, 5" × 5".

3 Draw a diagonal line from corner to corner on the wrong side of the remaining red A or B squares. Place a marked square on one corner of a tan piece, right sides together. Sew on the marked line. Trim the excess corner fabric ¼" from the stitched line. Place a marked square on the adjacent corner of the tan piece. Sew and trim as before to make a side unit measuring 3¼" × 5", including seam allowances. Make four units.

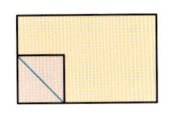

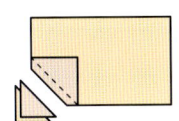

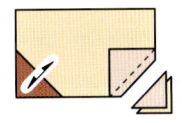

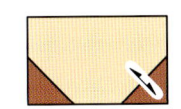

Make 4 units, 3¼" × 5".

4 Lay out four tan squares, the four side units, and the nine-patch unit in three rows. Sew the squares and units into rows. Join the rows to make a red Star block measuring 10½" square, including seam allowances. Repeat the steps to make 17 blocks.

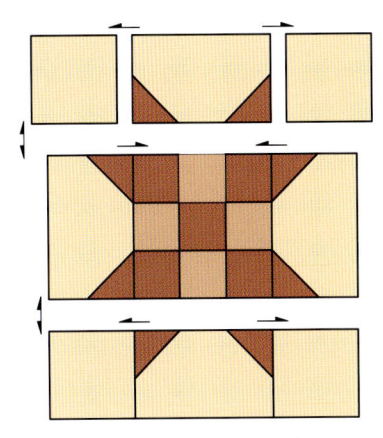

Make 17 red Star blocks, 10½" × 10½".

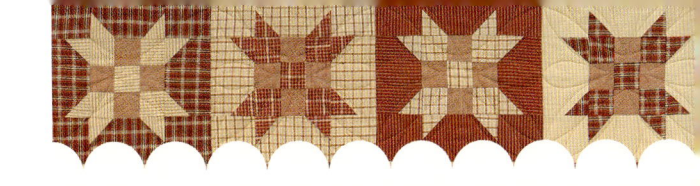

getting cozy with Lynne Hagmeier

If there's a chill in the air, I'm sure to have mushroom chicken rice in the oven.

When I'm ready to snuggle up with a quilt, I also need Netflix and the remote.

If I were the chancellor of Cozy College, my school uniform would be yoga pants and a T-shirt—my at-home work and play uniform.

Batting is the unseen hero in making a quilt cozy. Here's my choice for a quilt you can wrap up with: Warm & Natural 100% cotton.

If there's a bowl of popcorn and my favorite beverage, I'm having white cheddar cheese popcorn and black raspberry Ice.

When I'm curled under a quilt, the fabric backing is often just as visible to me as the top. So here's my tip for choosing backing fabric: I love flannel or brushed woven cotton plaids, and I try to choose a backing fabric that plays off the theme of the quilt.

For me, a quilt to curl up with has to at least wrap under my feet and over my shoulders. I'm tall, which is why my quilt in this book is 85" long!

My happy place to snuggle up with a quilt is by the fire pit in the fall or in my recliner.

Color has a vibe for many people. Other than the color combination I used in this book, a color combination that says "cozy" to me is greens with just about anything.

KTQuilts.com

cardinal crossing

assembling the quilt top

1. Referring to the quilt assembly diagram below, lay out the tan and red Star blocks in seven rows of five blocks each, alternating them in each row and from row to row. Sew the blocks into rows. Join the rows to make the quilt center, which should measure 50½" × 70½", including seam allowances.

2. Join the remaining red tone-on-tone strips end to end. From the pieced strip, cut two 70½"-long strips and two 53½"-long strips. Sew the longer strips to opposite sides of the quilt center. Sew the shorter strips to the top and bottom edges. Press all seam allowances toward the red strips. The quilt top should measure 53½" × 73½", including seam allowances.

3. Sew the red B 73½"-long strips to opposite sides of the quilt top. Sew the red B 65½"-long strips to the top and bottom edges. Press all seam allowances toward the outer border. The quilt top should measure 65½" × 85½".

finishing the quilt

For more details on any finishing steps, visit ShopMartingale.com/HowtoQuilt for free downloadable information.

1. Layer the quilt top with batting and backing; baste the layers together.

2. Quilt by hand or machine. Lynne's quilt is machine quilted with a loop design through the blocks. Ribbon candy is stitched in the inner border and parallel lines are stitched in the outer border.

3. Use the red B 2½"-wide strips to make double-fold binding and then attach the binding to the quilt.

Quilt assembly

snuggle up!

feeling leafy

The Maple Leaf block is one that Corey Yoder has used many times and in many lovely iterations. What's even more fun to snuggle under than a giant Maple Leaf block? A giant Maple Leaf block quilt with cozy Snuggles fabric by Moda as the backing. You may need to make more than one of this quilt to prevent dustups in the family room!

Designed and pieced by Corey Yoder; quilted by David Hurd

materials

Yardage is based on 42"-wide fabric unless otherwise indicated. Corey used Cozy Up by Corey Yoder for Moda Fabrics.

1½ yards of white print for block and border

34 squares, 10" × 10" *each*, of assorted prints for block and border

⅝ yard of gray diagonal stripe for binding

4 yards of cotton fabric OR 60"-wide Snuggles for backing

70" × 70" square of batting

cutting

All measurements include ¼" seam allowances.

From the white print, cut:
- 1 strip, 10" × 42"; crosscut into 4 squares, 10" × 10"
- 3 strips, 9½" × 42"; crosscut into 11 squares, 9½" × 9½"
- 1 strip, 8½" × 42"; crosscut into 4 squares, 8½" × 8½"

From *each* of 30 assorted print squares, cut:
- 1 square, 9½" × 9½" (30 total)

From the gray diagonal stripe, cut:
- 7 strips, 2½" × 42"

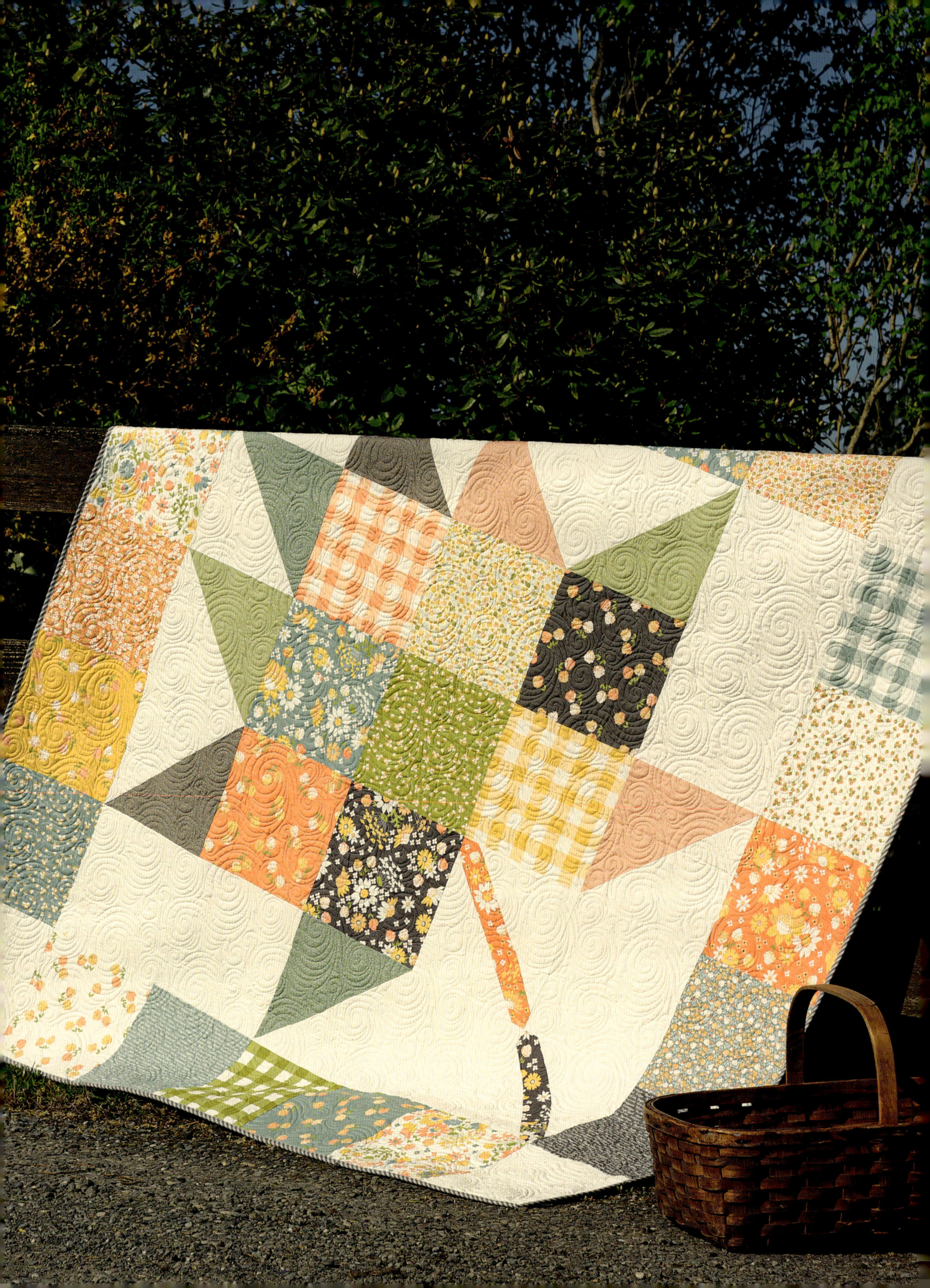

making the block

Press seam allowances in the directions indicated by the arrows.

1 Draw a diagonal line from corner to corner on the wrong side of the white 10" squares. Layer a marked square on a print 10" square, right sides together. Sew ¼" from both sides of the drawn line. Cut the unit apart on the marked line to make two half-square-triangle units. Trim the units to 9½" square, including seam allowances. Make eight units.

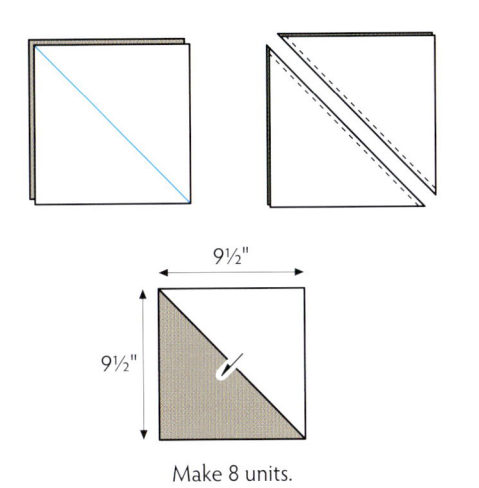

Make 8 units.

2 Draw a diagonal line from corner to corner on the wrong side of the white 8½" squares. Place a marked square on one corner of a print 9½" square, right sides together. Sew on the marked line. Trim the excess corner fabric ¼" from the stitched line. Place a marked square on the opposite corner of the print square. Sew and trim as before to make a stem unit measuring 9½" square, including seam allowances. Make two stem units.

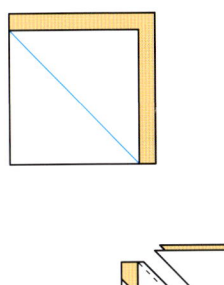

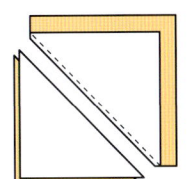

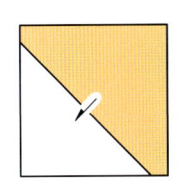

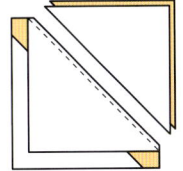

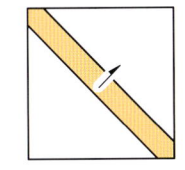

Make 2 units, 9½" × 9½".

feeling leafy ♥ 15

FINISHED QUILT:
63½" × 63½"
FINISHED BLOCK:
45" × 45"

3. Lay out seven white 9½" squares, eight print 9½" squares, the half-square-triangle units, and the stem units in five rows, noting the orientation of the triangle and stem units. Sew the squares and units into rows. Join the rows to make a block measuring 45½" square, including seam allowances.

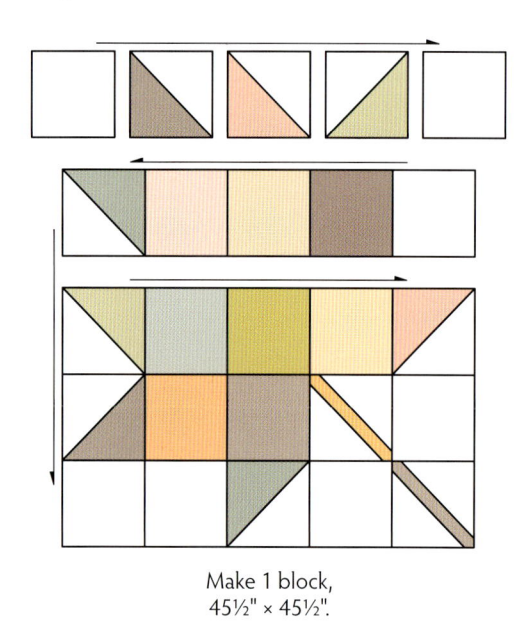

Make 1 block,
45½" × 45½".

assembling the quilt top

1. Referring to the quilt assembly diagram on page 17, join five print 9½" squares to make a side border that measures 9½" × 45½", including seam allowances. Make two. Make two more borders in the same way and add a white 9½" square to each end. The top and bottom borders should measure 9½" × 63½", including seam allowances.

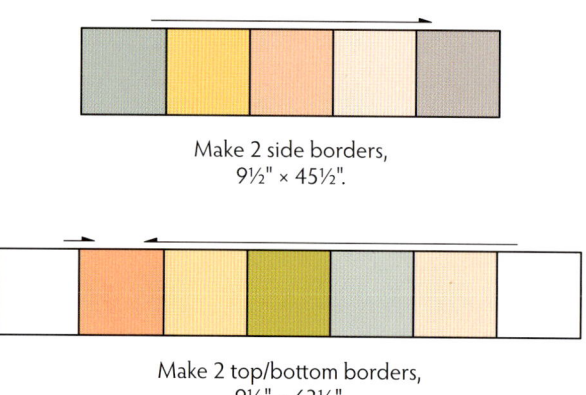

Make 2 side borders,
9½" × 45½".

Make 2 top/bottom borders,
9½" × 63½".

16 ♥ snuggle up!

2. Sew the short borders to the left and right edges of the block and then sew the longer borders to the top and bottom edges. The quilt top should measure 63½" square.

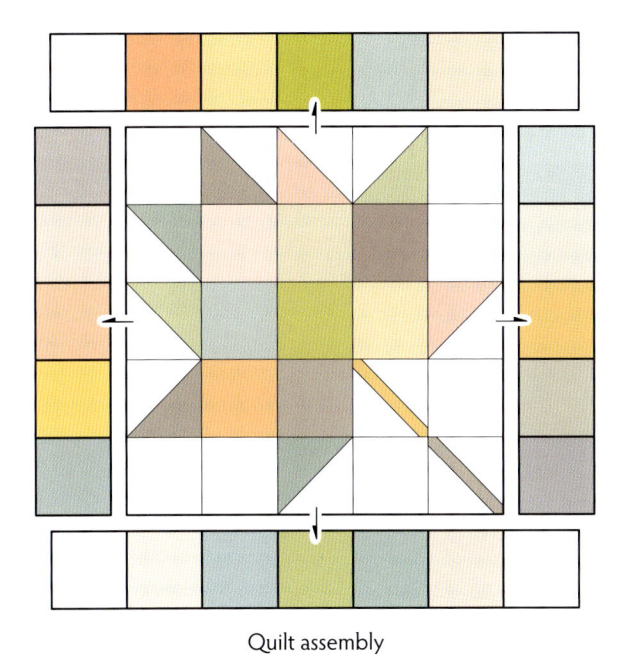

Quilt assembly

finishing the quilt

For more details on any finishing steps, visit ShopMartingale.com/HowtoQuilt for free downloadable information.

1. Layer the quilt top with batting and backing; baste the layers together.
2. Quilt by hand or machine. Corey's quilt is machine quilted with an allover swirl design.
3. Use the gray 2½"-wide strips to make double-fold binding and then attach the binding to the quilt.

getting cozy with Corey Yoder

If there's a chill in the air, I'm sure to have a yummy soup on the stove.

When I'm ready to snuggle up with a quilt, I also need a good book.

If I were the chancellor of Cozy College, my school uniform would be soft pants and a T-shirt.

Batting is the unseen hero in making a quilt cozy. Here's my choice for a quilt you can wrap up with: I always leave this up to my quilter. My only request is for low-loft.

If there's a bowl of popcorn and my favorite beverage, I'm having caramel corn and chai (or a chai latte if I'm feeling extra festive!).

When I'm curled under a quilt, the fabric backing is often just as visible to me as the top. So here's my tip for choosing backing fabric: For a truly cuddly quilt, Minky or Snuggles by Moda is the way to go. These are the ones my family fights over.

For me, a quilt to curl up with has to at least cover me from neck to toes.

My happy place to snuggle up with a quilt is any place where I can snuggle with family.

Color has a vibe for many people. Other than the color combination I used in this book, a color combination that says "cozy" to me is grays and warm whites.

CorianderQuilts.com

feeling leafy 17

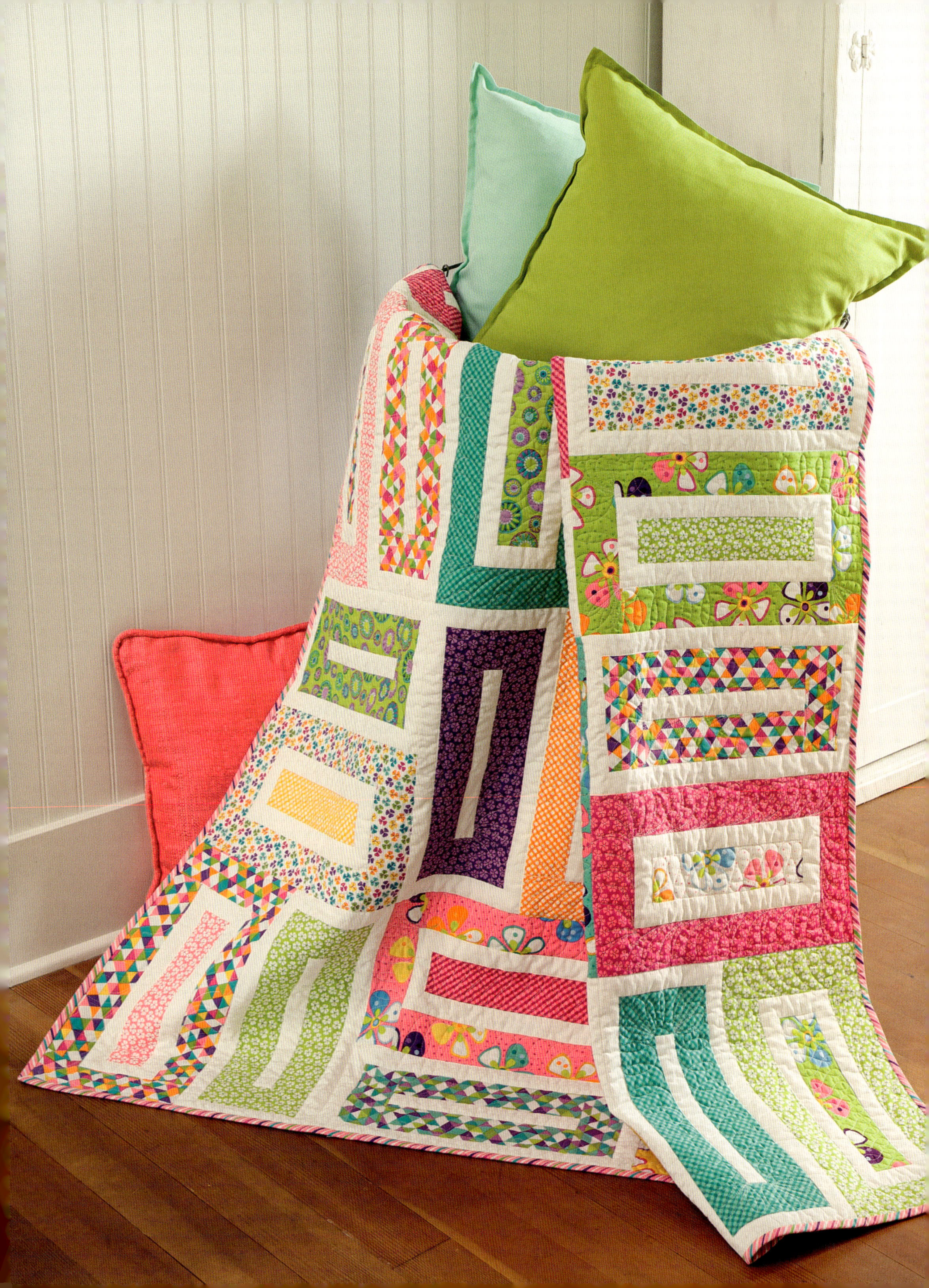

rolling pins

Trust us—sisters Barbara Groves and Mary Jacobson have created Rolling Pin blocks that are easier than rolling out a perfect pie crust! You'll join two long, skinny log-cabin units to make each block. And the beauty is, you never have to match up seamlines, so sewing the blocks together couldn't be simpler.

Designed and pieced by Barbara Groves and Mary Jacobson; quilted by Sharon Elsberry

materials

Yardage is based on 42"-wide fabric. Fat quarters measure 18" × 21". Barb and Mary used Petal Power by Me and My Sister Designs for Moda Fabrics.

2 yards of white print for blocks

20 fat quarters of assorted prints for blocks

⅝ yard of pink diagonal stripe for binding

4⅝ yards of fabric for backing

67" × 82" piece of batting

cutting

All measurements include ¼" seam allowances.

From the white print, cut:
- 43 strips, 1½" × 42"; crosscut into:
    40 strips, 1½" × 13½"
    60 strips, 1½" × 9½"
    40 strips, 1½" × 7½"
    40 strips, 1½" × 4½"

From *each* of the assorted prints, cut:
- 2 strips, 2½" × 11½" (40 total)
- 3 strips, 2½" × 9½" (60 total)
- 2 strips, 2½" × 8½" (40 total)
- 2 strips, 2½" × 5½" (40 total)

From the pink diagonal stripe, cut:
- 8 strips, 2½" × 42"

making the blocks

Press seam allowances in the directions indicated by the arrows.

1. Sew white 1½" × 9½" strips to the long edges of a print 2½" × 9½" strip. Sew white 1½" × 4½" strips to the ends of the unit. It should measure 4½" × 11½", including seam allowances. Make 20 units.

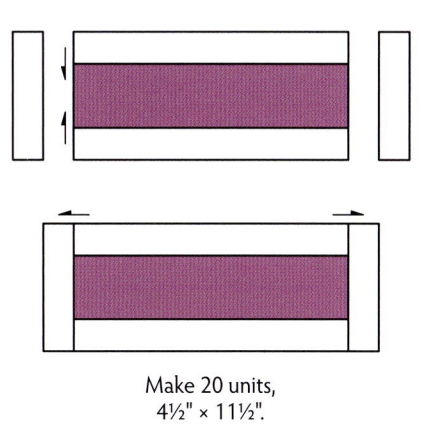

Make 20 units, 4½" × 11½".

FINISHED QUILT:
60½" × 75½"

FINISHED BLOCK:
15" × 15"

20 ♥ *snuggle up!*

2 Using the matching strips from a different print, sew print 2½" × 11½" strips to the long edges of a unit from step 1. Sew print 2½" × 8½" strips to the ends of the unit to make unit A. It should measure 8½" × 15½", including seam allowances. Make 20 units.

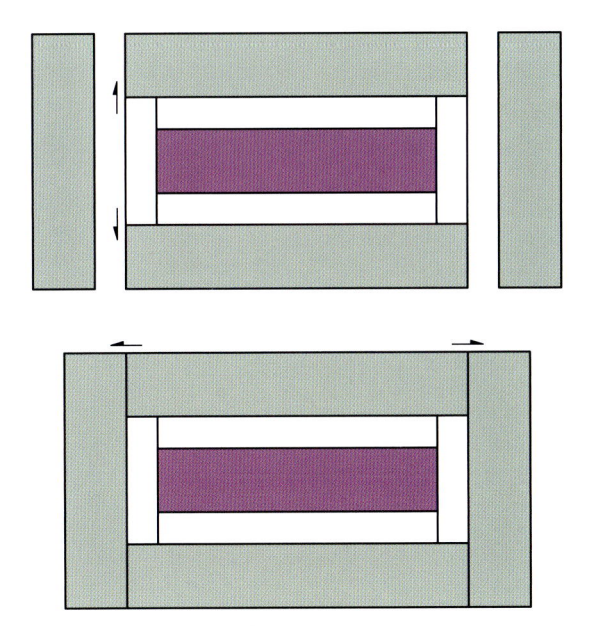

Make 20 A units,
8½" × 15½".

3 Using one print throughout this step, sew print 2½" × 9½" strips to the long edges of a white 1½" × 9½" strip. Sew print 2½" × 5½" strips to the ends of the unit. It should measure 5½" × 13½", including seam allowances. Make 20 units.

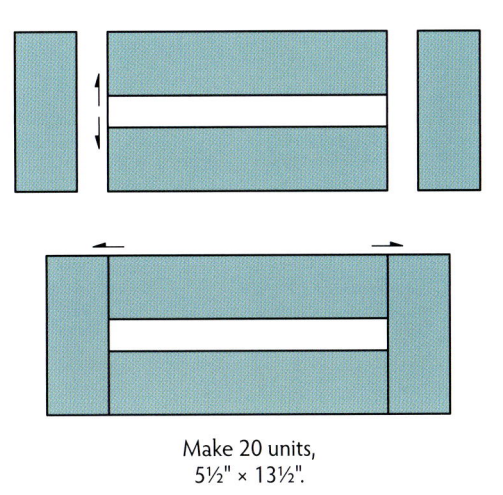

Make 20 units,
5½" × 13½".

FAUX BIAS BINDING

Stripes on the diagonal give a perfect finishing touch to a quilt. But don't go to the trouble of cutting and making bias binding to create this effect. Simply look for a stripe that's printed diagonally. You can cut binding strips across the fabric width, and the diagonal stripes do the work!

4 Sew white 1½" × 13½" strips to the long edges of a unit from step 3. Sew white 1½" × 7½" strips to the ends of the unit to make unit B. It should measure 7½" × 15½", including seam allowances. Make 20 units.

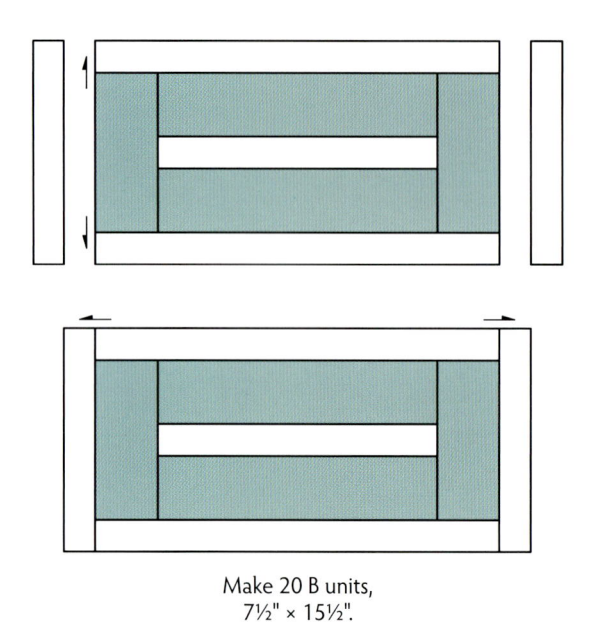

Make 20 B units,
7½" × 15½".

5 Join one A unit and one B unit to make a block measuring 15½" square, including seam allowances. Make 20 blocks.

Make 20 blocks,
15½" × 15½".

assembling the quilt top

Lay out the blocks in five rows of four blocks each, rotating them as shown in the quilt assembly diagram. Sew the blocks into rows. Join the rows to complete the quilt top. The quilt top should measure 60½" × 75½".

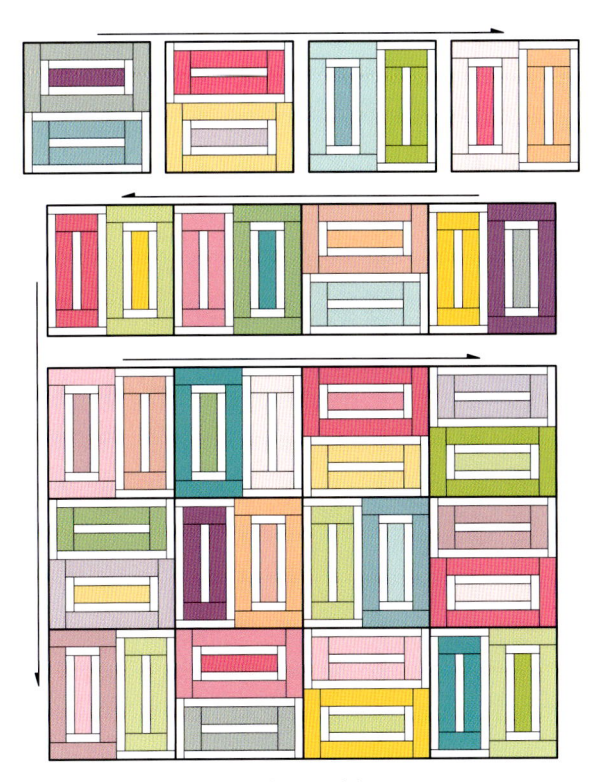

Quilt assembly

finishing the quilt

For more details on any finishing steps, visit ShopMartingale.com/HowtoQuilt for free downloadable information.

1. Layer the quilt top with batting and backing; baste the layers together.

2. Quilt by hand or machine. Barbara and Mary's quilt is machine quilted in the ditch along the seamlines. Ribbon candy, feathers, and loops are stitched in the print areas of the blocks.

3. Use the pink 2½"-wide strips to make double-fold binding and then attach the binding to the quilt.

getting cozy with Barbara Groves

If there's a chill in the air, I'm sure to have soup in the slow cooker.

When I'm ready to snuggle up with a quilt, I also need the remote control to watch my giant TV.

If I were the chancellor of Cozy College, my school uniform would be stretchy pants.

Batting is the unseen hero in making a quilt cozy. Here's my choice for a quilt you can wrap up with: Quilters Dream.

If there's a bowl of popcorn and my favorite beverage, I'm having something a little different. Currently I'm on a chocolate-covered raisin jag, and I'm sipping hot tea or diet ginger ale.

When I'm curled under a quilt, the fabric backing is often just as visible to me as the top. So here's my tip for choosing backing fabric: Make it as good as the front, with fabric you love, and piece in any leftover blocks.

For me, a quilt to curl up with has to at least cover my chin down to my wrapped-up toes.

My happy place to snuggle up with a quilt is in my bed or sewing room chair, with at least three pillows.

Color has a vibe for many people. Other than the color combination I used in this book, a color combination that says "cozy" to me is simple, scrappy green plaid squares.

MeandMySisterDesigns.com

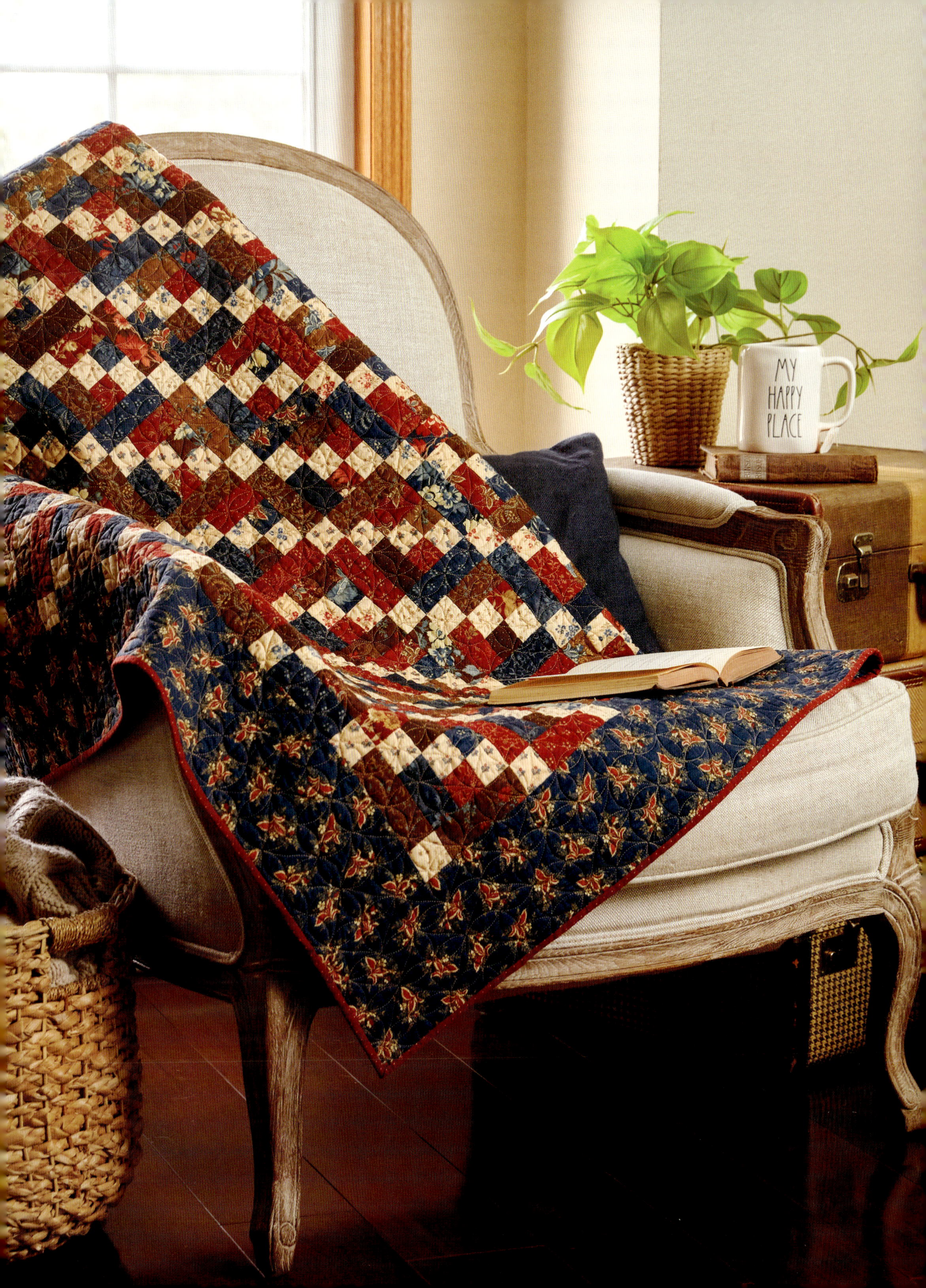
MY
HAPPY
PLACE

boardwalk

Strategically placed light-colored squares mark the diagonal pathway across this quilt top, but there are no diagonal seams to be found! Easy units stitched from simple squares and rectangles will have you skipping along the boardwalk in no time.

Designed and pieced by Betsy Chutchian; quilted by Maggi Honeyman

materials

Yardage is based on 42"-wide fabric. Fat eighths measure 9" × 21". Betsy used Maria's Sky by Betsy Chutchian for Moda Fabrics.

25 fat eighths of assorted medium and dark prints (collectively referred to as "dark") for blocks and inner border

¼ yard *each* of 4 assorted light prints for blocks and inner border

⅞ yard of navy floral for outer border

½ yard of dark red print for binding

2¾ yards of fabric for backing

48" × 58" piece of batting

cutting

All measurements include ¼" seam allowances.

From *each* of the assorted dark prints, cut:
- 3 strips, 1¾" × 21"; crosscut into:
    5 strips, 1¾" × 4¼" (125 total; 15 are extra)
    4 pieces, 1¾" × 3" (100 total; 4 are extra)
    4 squares, 1¾" × 1¾" (100 total; 4 are extra)

From *each* of the assorted light prints, cut:
- 3 strips, 1¾" × 42"; crosscut into 52 squares, 1¾" × 1¾" (208 total; 1 is extra)

From the navy floral, cut:
- 5 strips, 5½" × 42"

From the dark red print, cut:
- 5 strips, 2½" × 42"

making the blocks

Directions are for making one block. Repeat to make a total of 48 blocks. Press seam allowances in the directions indicated by the arrows.

1. Lay out two matching light squares and two different dark squares in two rows of two. Sew the squares into rows. Join the rows to make a four-patch unit measuring 3" square, including seam allowances.

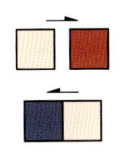

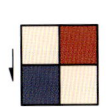

Make 1 unit, 3" × 3".

FINISHED QUILT:
41¾" × 51¾"
FINISHED BLOCK:
5" × 5"

26 ♥ snuggle up!

2. Lay out one light square, two dark 1¾" × 3" pieces, and the four-patch unit in two rows as shown. The light square should match the four-patch unit. Sew into rows and then join the rows. The unit should measure 4¼" square, including seam allowances.

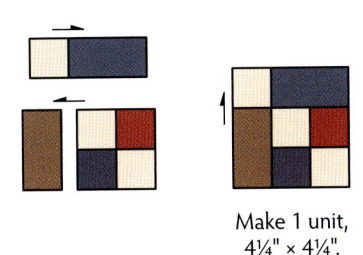

Make 1 unit, 4¼" × 4¼".

3. Lay out one matching light square, two dark 1¾" × 4¼" strips, and the unit from step 2 in two rows as shown. Sew into rows and then join the rows to make a block measuring 5½" square, including seam allowances. Repeat the steps to make a total of 48 blocks.

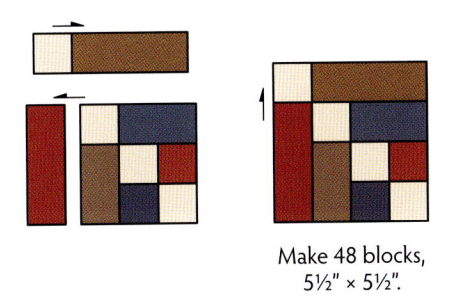

Make 48 blocks, 5½" × 5½".

assembling the quilt top

1. Sew a light square to the end of a dark 1¾" × 4¼" strip. Repeat to make 14 border units measuring 1¾" × 5½", including seam allowances.

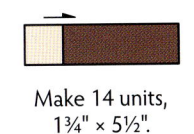

Make 14 units, 1¾" × 5½".

2. Referring to the quilt assembly diagram on page 28, lay out the blocks in eight rows of six blocks each on a design wall or floor. Add a border unit from step 1 to the end of each row as shown. Notice that in the quilt on page 26, the light square in each border unit matches the light print in the previous row to form a diagonal row of five matching squares.

getting cozy with Betsy Chutchian

If there's a chill in the air, I'm sure to have a roast in the oven or a pot of chili on the stove.

When I'm ready to snuggle up with a quilt, I also need the TV remote.

If I were the chancellor of Cozy College, my school uniform would be leggings and a soft oversized but cute top or hoodie.

Batting is the unseen hero in making a quilt cozy. Here's my choice for a quilt you can wrap up with: 100% cotton. I love how it drapes.

If there's a bowl of popcorn and my favorite beverage, I'm having buttered popcorn, slices of cheddar cheese, a dill pickle, and a Coke.

When I'm curled under a quilt, the fabric backing is often just as visible to me as the top. So here's my tip for choosing backing fabric: Choose a backing fabric you love. I once overheard a mom and daughter at the quilt shop where I worked years ago. Mom wanted the backing to match. Daughter wanted something special, because when she covers up, that fabric goes next to her. I've never forgotten that conversation.

For me, a quilt to curl up with has to at least cover my lap.

My happy place to snuggle up with a quilt is on my living room couch.

Color has a vibe for many people. Other than the color combination I used in this book, a color combination that says "cozy" to me is varied. I change out quilts for the couch per season or holiday, so cozy is whatever is currently on the couch!

BetsysBestQuiltsandMore.blogspot.com

5 Sew the border to the bottom edge of the quilt top. The quilt top should measure 31¾" × 41¾", including seam allowances.

6 Join the navy strips end to end. From the pieced strip, cut four 41¾"-long strips. Sew strips to the left and right edges of the quilt center. Sew the remaining strips to the top and bottom edges. The quilt top should measure 41¾" × 51¾".

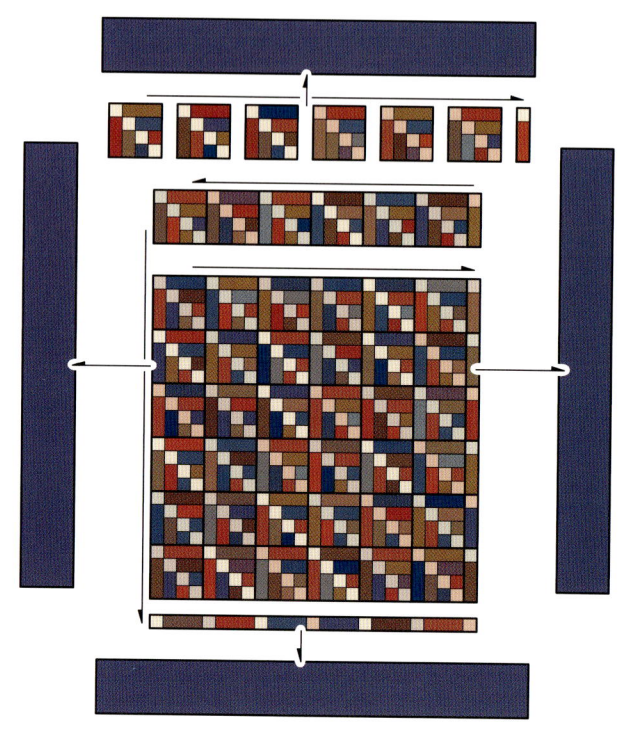

Quilt assembly

3 Sew the blocks and units into rows. Join the rows to make the quilt center, which should measure 31¾" × 40½", including seam allowances.

4 Lay out six border units and one light square to make a bottom border. When sewn to the quilt top, the light squares in the bottom border should complete the diagonal rows of matching squares. Join the pieces to make a border measuring 1¾" × 31¾", including seam allowances.

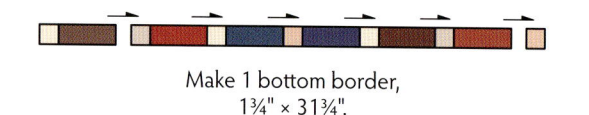

Make 1 bottom border, 1¾" × 31¾".

finishing the quilt

For more details on any finishing steps, visit ShopMartingale.com/HowtoQuilt for free downloadable information.

1 Layer the quilt top with batting and backing; baste the layers together.

2 Quilt by hand or machine. Betsy's quilt is machine quilted with an allover pumpkin seed design.

3 Use the dark red 2½"-wide strips to make binding and then attach the binding to the quilt.

♥ snuggle up!

sprightly

While the definition of *sprightly* is "lively and full of spirit,"
that doesn't mean this quilt isn't perfect for some downtime too!
Sprightly is just the right size for a tall friend who wants to enjoy a nap
on the couch or even two friends who want to snuggle together.
A Jelly Roll provides a head start on making this quick, cuddly quilt.

*Designed by Linzee Kull McCray and Pam Ehrhardt;
pieced and quilted by Pam Ehrhardt*

materials

Yardage is based on 42"-wide fabric. Linzee used Flowers for Freya by Linzee Kull McCray for Moda Fabrics.

1 Jelly Roll, which is 42 strips, 2½" × 42" *each*, of assorted prints for blocks and binding

4½ yards of white print for blocks, sashing, and setting triangles

1 yard of teal print for sashing and border

4½ yards of fabric for backing

79" × 79" square of batting

Template plastic or Strip Tube Junior ruler by Cozy Quilt Designs

cutting

Before you begin, set aside 18 of the darkest print strips for making half-square-triangle units (see page 31). Set aside 8 assorted print strips for binding. All measurements include ¼" seam allowances.

From *each* of 15 of the remaining print strips, cut:
- 2 strips, 2½" × 21" (30 total; 1 is extra)

From the white print, cut:
- 2 strips, 16" × 42"; crosscut into:
    3 squares, 16" × 16"; cut the squares into quarters diagonally to yield 12 side triangles
    2 squares, 8¼" × 8¼"; cut the squares in half diagonally to yield 4 corner triangles
- 45 strips, 2½" × 42"; crosscut *27 of the strips* into:
    4 strips, 2½" × 21"
    64 strips, 2½" × 10½"
    100 squares, 2½" × 2½"

From the teal print, cut:
- 1 strip, 3¼" × 42"; crosscut into 8 squares, 3¼" × 3¼". Cut the squares in half diagonally to yield 16 triangles.
- 10 strips, 2½" × 42"; crosscut *2 of the strips* into 24 squares, 2½" × 2½"

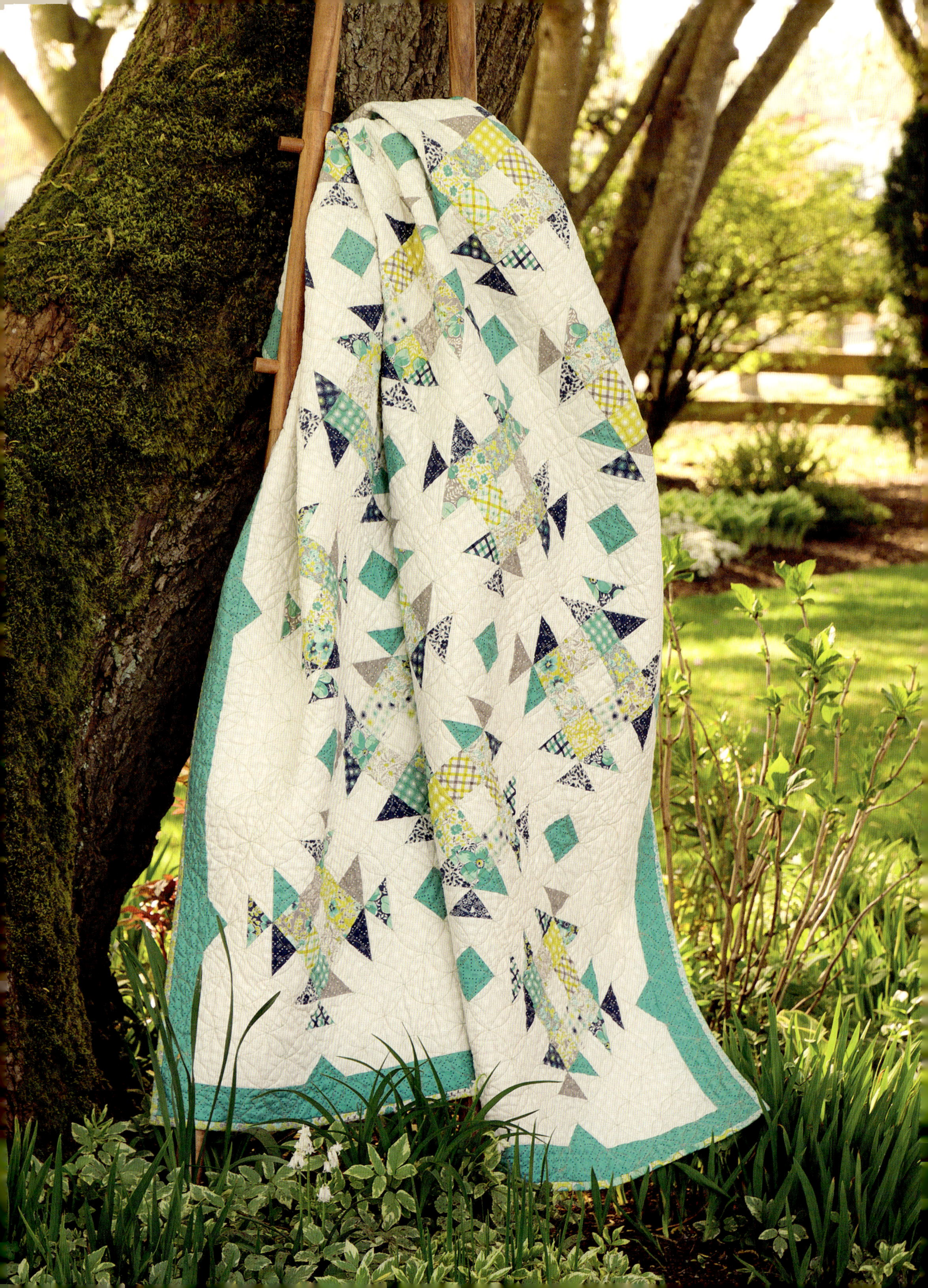

making the half-square-triangle units

Press seam allowances in the directions indicated by the arrows.

1. If you're not using the Strip Tube Junior ruler, you'll need to make a triangle-cutting template. To make a template, trace the triangle pattern on page 35 onto template plastic. Use utility scissors to cut out the template *exactly* on the drawn lines.

2. Layer one print 2½" × 42" strip and one white 2½" × 42" strip right sides together. Sew along both long edges using a consistent ¼" seam allowance. Make 18 strip sets.

Make 18 strip sets.

3. With the white strip on top, align the long side of the triangle template with the bottom edge of the strip set. Cut along both angled sides of the template or ruler to release a triangle unit. Rotate the template, align the angled edge with the newly cut edge, and align the long side of the template with the top edge of the strip set. Cut along the right edge of the template to make a triangle. (If you're using a ruler, align the 3" line on the ruler with the stitched line along the bottom or top of the strip set.) Cut 17 triangles from each strip set (306 total). You'll have six extra units.

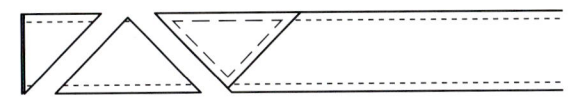

Cut 17 triangles from each strip set (306 total).

4. Press and trim the units to 2½" square, including seam allowances. Make 300 units.

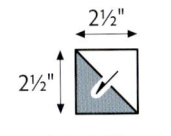

2½"
2½"

Make 300 units.

HANDLE WITH CARE

Using this strip method is fast and lets you make good use of your fabric strips. But, the outside edges of the half-square-triangle units will be on the bias. Handle them with care while sewing and pressing so as not to distort the blocks.

making the nine-patch units

1. Join three different print 2½" × 21" strips to make a strip set A measuring 6½" × 21". Make six more of strip set A. Cut the strip sets into 50 segments, 2½" × 6½". Cut the strip sets carefully; you will not have any leftover fabric.

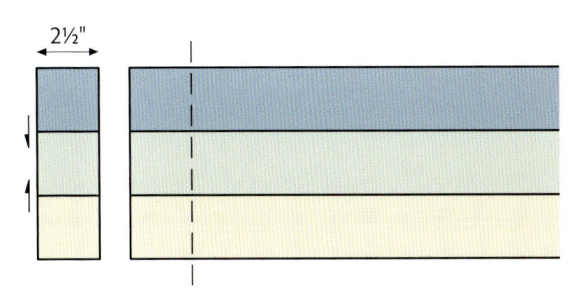

2½"

Make 7 A strip sets, 6½" × 21".
Cut 50 segments, 2½" × 6½".

sprightly ♥ 31

FINISHED QUILT:
72½" × 72½"

FINISHED BLOCK:
10" × 10"

32 ♥ snuggle up!

2 Join two different print 2½" × 21" strips to opposite sides of a white 2½" × 21" strip to make a strip set B measuring 6½" × 21". Make four of strip set B. Cut the strip sets into 25 segments, 2½" × 6½".

Make 4 B strip sets, 6½" × 21".
Cut 25 segments, 2½" × 6½".

3 Join two A segments and one B segment to make a nine-patch unit. Make 25 units measuring 6½" square, including seam allowances.

Make 25 units, 6½" × 6½".

making the blocks

1 Join four half-square-triangle units and one white 2½" square to make a unit measuring 2½" × 10½", including seam allowances. Make 50 units.

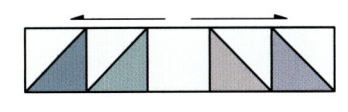

Make 50 units, 2½" × 10½".

2 Join two half-square-triangle units and one white 2½" square to make a unit measuring 2½" × 6½", including seam allowances. Make 50 units.

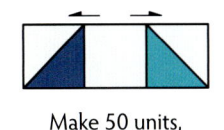

Make 50 units, 2½" × 6½".

getting cozy with Linzee Kull McCray

If there's a chill in the air, I'm sure to have soup! I love so many kinds of soup, from chicken and wild rice to butternut squash to chili. It warms me up from the inside!

When I'm ready to snuggle up with a quilt, I also need one of the hundreds of books from my Goodreads list.

If I were the chancellor of Cozy College, my school uniform would be a cozy top, a scarf, and leggings with pockets. The pandemic taught me that there's really no reason to wear anything else in the winter.

Batting is the unseen hero in making a quilt cozy. Here's my choice for a quilt you can wrap up with: Team Wool batting all the way! I love it for winter and summer quilts (it's so lightweight and never seems too hot).

If there's a bowl of popcorn and my favorite beverage, I'm having salty popcorn. My drink of choice is a *pamplemousse* (grapefruit) LaCroix.

When I'm curled under a quilt, the fabric backing is often just as visible to me as the top. So here's my tip for choosing backing fabric: I'm a fan of pieced backings. Once I used 40 fabrics in a quilt and made a "key" on the back—a 2" square of every fabric, set off by sashing—as part of a pieced back.

For me, a quilt to curl up with has to at least be long enough for my husband (he's 6' 5"), which means it covers me from my chin to my toes.

My happy place to snuggle up with a quilt is either my couch or my bed.

Color has a vibe for many people. Other than the color combination I used in this book, a color combination that says "cozy" to me is oranges, yellows, and reds.

LinzeeKullMcCray.com

3 Lay out two units from step 1, two units from step 2, and one nine-patch unit in three rows, noting the orientation of the dark triangles. Sew the units from step 2 to the left and right sides of the nine-patch unit. Join the rows to make a block measuring 10½" square, including seam allowances. Make 25 blocks.

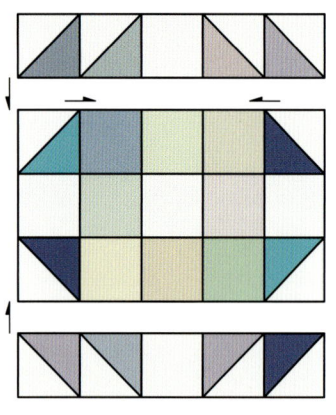

Make 25 blocks, 10½" × 10½".

assembling the quilt top

1 Lay out the blocks, white 2½" × 10½" strips, teal squares and triangles, and white side and corner triangles in diagonal rows as shown in the quilt assembly diagram below. Join the white strips, teal squares, and teal triangles to make sashing rows. Sew the blocks and white strips into rows to make block rows. Sew a sashing row to the top of each appropriate block row, and then add the white side triangles. Join the rows, adding the corner triangles last.

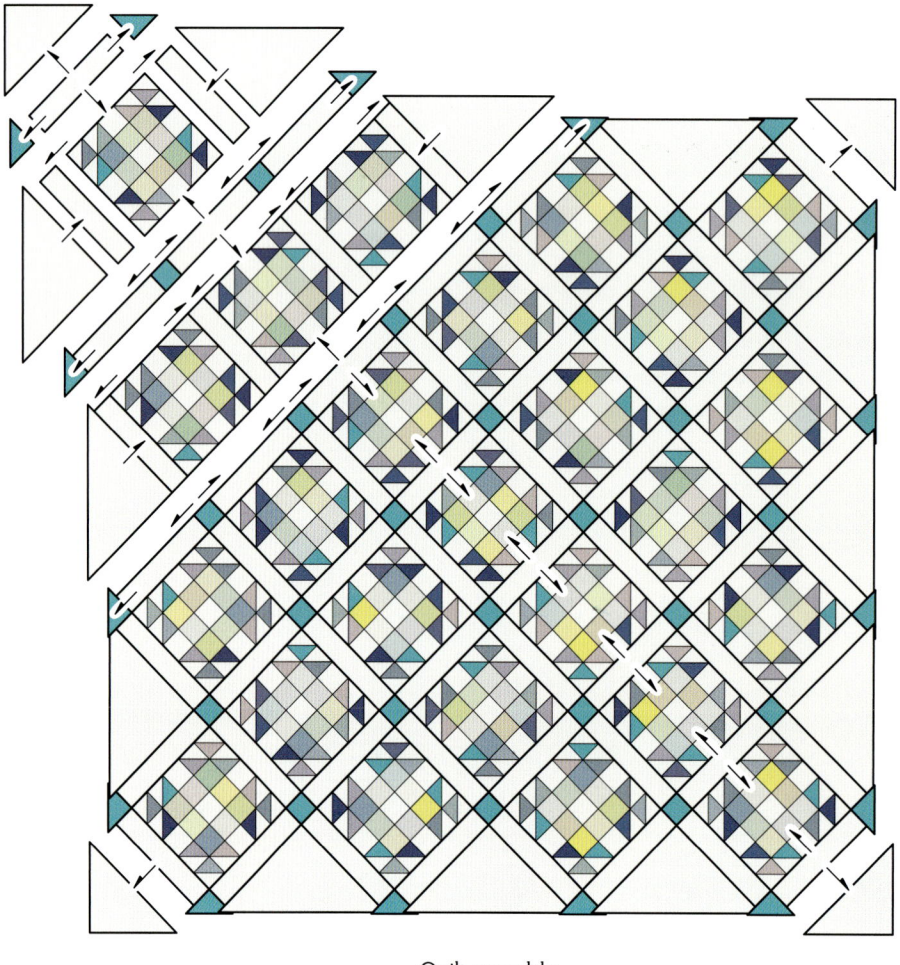

Quilt assembly

2. Trim and square up the quilt top, making sure to leave ¼" beyond the points of the sashing strips for seam allowances. The quilt-top center should measure 68½" square, including seam allowances.

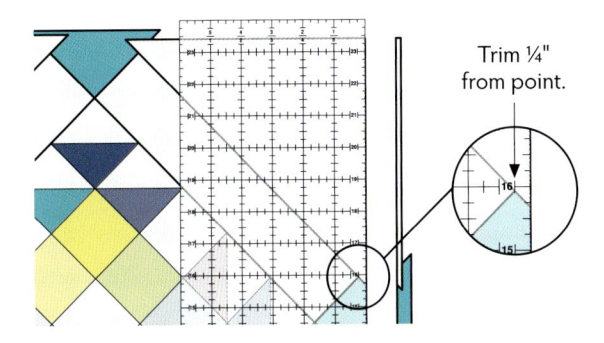

Trim ¼" from point.

3. Join eight teal 2½"-wide strips end to end. From the pieced strip, cut two 72½"-long strips and two 68½"-long strips. Sew the shorter strips to opposite sides of the quilt center. Sew the longer strips to the top and bottom edges. Press all seam allowances toward the outer border. The quilt top should measure 72½" square.

finishing the quilt

For more details on any finishing steps, visit ShopMartingale.com/HowtoQuilt for free downloadable information.

1. Layer the quilt top with batting and backing; baste the layers together.

2. Quilt by hand or machine. Linzee's quilt is machine quilted with an allover pumpkin seed design.

3. Use the remaining print 2½"-wide strips to make binding and then attach the binding to the quilt.

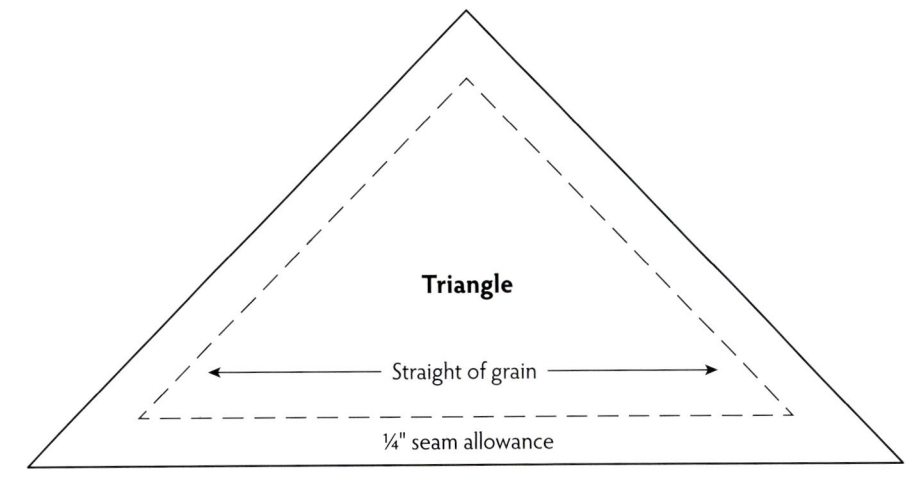

Triangle

Straight of grain

¼" seam allowance

sprightly 35

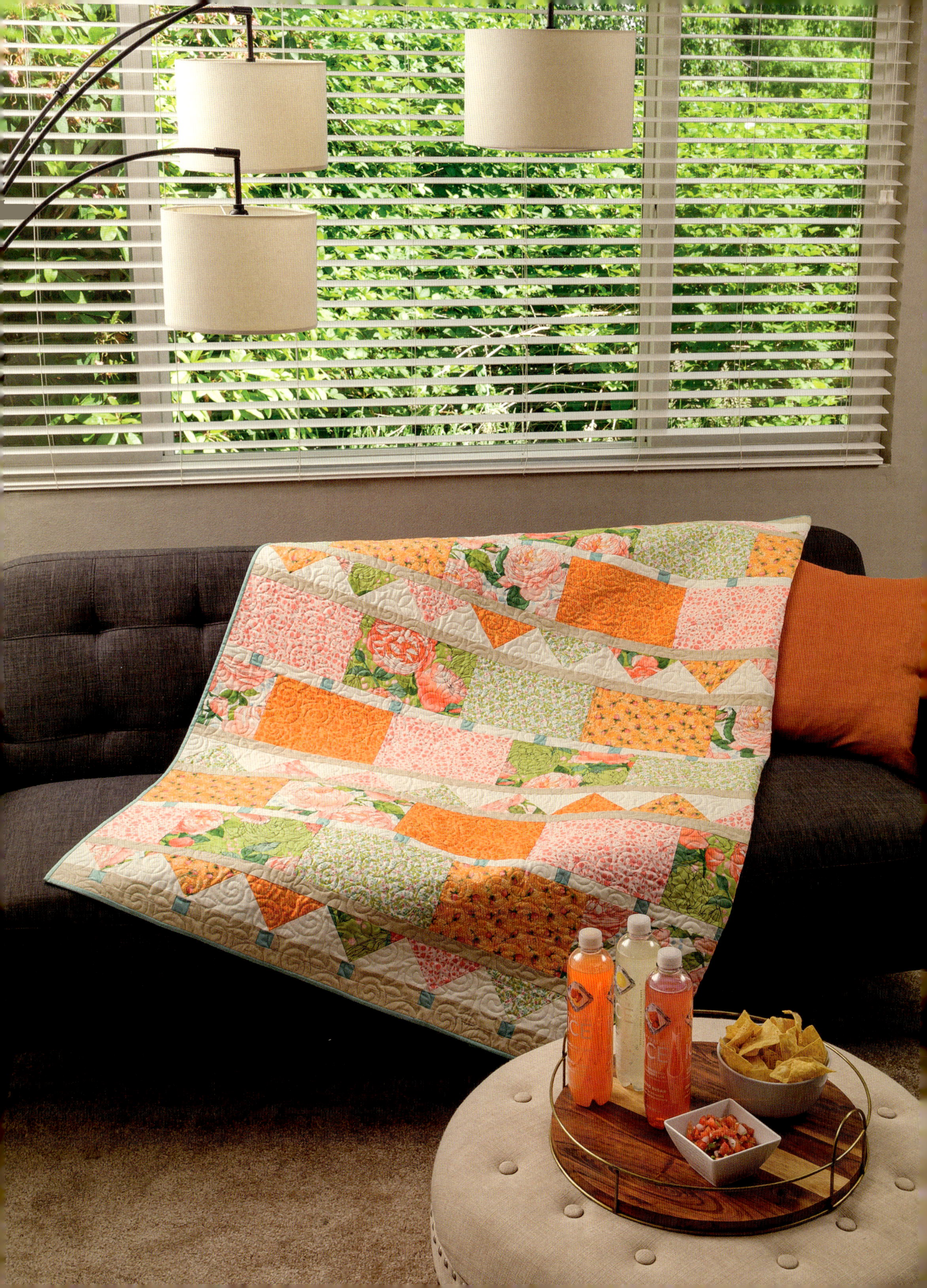

good fences, good neighbors

Built-in rows, just like good fences, create friendly vibes in this fun-to-stitch quilt. The design is ideal for showcasing a favorite collection of fabrics in large rectangles and flying-geese units. Pops of high-contrast little squares add to the appeal of this pattern.

Designed, pieced, and quilted by Robin Pickens

materials

Yardage is based on 42"-wide fabric. Robin used Abby Rose and Thatched (tone on tones), both by Robin Pickens for Moda Fabrics.

1⅛ yards of cream tone on tone for flying-geese units and sashing

⅝ yard *each* of 6 assorted prints in orange, pink, and green for flying-geese units and rows

¾ yard of taupe tone on tone for sashing and border

¾ yard of teal tone on tone for accent squares and binding

3¾ yards of fabric for backing

67" × 68" piece of batting

cutting

All measurements include ¼" seam allowances.

From the cream tone on tone, cut:
- 8 strips, 3½" × 42"; crosscut into 80 squares, 3½" × 3½"
- 5 strips, 1½" × 42"; crosscut into:
    27 pieces, 1½" × 5½"
    6 pieces, 1½" × 3"

From *each* of 3 assorted prints, cut:
- 2 strips, 6½" × 42"; crosscut into:
    6 pieces, 6½" × 10½" (18 total)
    4 pieces, 3½" × 6½" (12 total)
- 1 strip, 3½" × 42"; crosscut into 3 pieces, 3½" × 6½" (9 total; 1 is extra)

From *each* of the remaining 3 assorted prints, cut:
- 2 strips, 6½" × 42"; crosscut into:
    5 pieces, 6½" × 10½" (15 total)
    2 pieces, 5½" × 6½" (6 total)
    4 pieces, 3½" × 6½" (12 total)
- 1 strip, 3½" × 42"; crosscut into 3 pieces, 3½" × 6½" (9 total; 1 is extra)

From the taupe tone on tone, cut:
- 16 strips, 1½" × 42"; crosscut *3 of the strips* into:
    18 pieces, 1½" × 5½"
    4 pieces, 1½" × 3"

From the teal tone on tone, cut:
- 7 strips, 2½" × 42"
- 2 strips, 1½" × 42"; crosscut into 50 squares, 1½" × 1½"

FINISHED QUILT:
60½" × 61½"

38 ♥ snuggle up!

assembling the quilt top

Press seam allowances in the directions indicated by the arrows.

1 Draw a diagonal line from corner to corner on the wrong side of the cream 3½" squares. Place a marked square on one end of a print 3½" × 6½" piece, right sides together. Sew on the marked line. Trim the excess corner fabric ¼" from the stitched line. Place a marked square on the opposite end of the print piece. Sew and trim as before to make a flying-geese unit measuring 3½" × 6½", including seam allowances. Make 40 units.

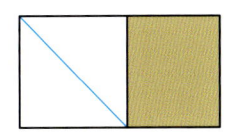

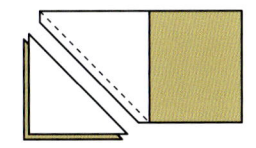

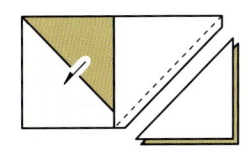

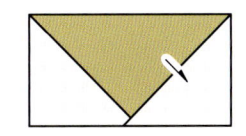

Make 40 units,
3½" × 6½".

2 Join 10 flying-geese units end to end to make a row measuring 3½" × 60½", including seam allowances. Make four of row A.

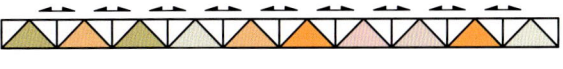

Make 4 A rows,
3½" × 60½".

3 Randomly join six print 6½" × 10½" pieces to make a row measuring 6½" × 60½", including seam allowances. Make three of row B.

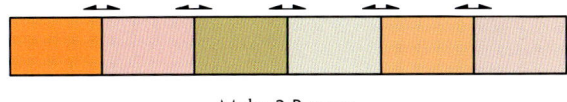

Make 3 B rows,
6½" × 60½".

getting cozy with
Robin Pickens

If there's a chill in the air, I'm sure to have brownies in the oven or chili on the stove.

When I'm ready to snuggle up with a quilt, I also need my furry friend Roxy, my labradoodle who must be around me at all times.

If I were the chancellor of Cozy College, my school uniform would be leggings with a quilt-themed T-shirt, of course!

Batting is the unseen hero in making a quilt cozy. Here's my choice for a quilt you can wrap up with: Warm & Natural is my go-to batting, but I'm experimenting with Kyoto bamboo and Hobbs silk batting too.

If there's a bowl of popcorn and my favorite beverage, I'm having Orville Redenbacher's Naturals Simply Salted microwave popcorn and a black cherry seltzer.

When I'm curled under a quilt, the fabric backing is often just as visible to me as the top. So here's my tip for choosing backing fabric: I love backing that brings out an accent color from the quilt top! I'm thrilled with my new 108"-wide Thatched backings—so soft!

For me, a quilt to curl up with has to at least cover my lap, with room for my dog to sit on it.

My happy place to snuggle up with a quilt is on the couch in my family room. But I've been known to take quilts along when waiting in the car on chilly evenings while my son was in youth orchestra practice.

Color has a vibe for many people. Other than the color combination I used in this book, a color combination that says "cozy" to me is anything with my Washed Linen Thatched fabrics. It's such a nice light neutral and it makes quilts look warm and comfy.

RobinPickens.com

4 Join two print 5½" × 6½" pieces and five print 6½" × 10½" pieces to make a row measuring 6½" × 60½", including seam allowances. Notice that Robin used the same print on both ends of the row. Make three of row C.

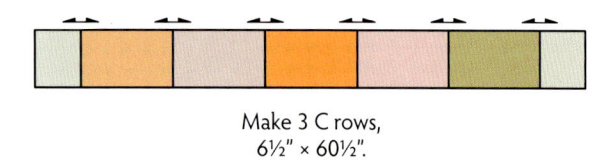

Make 3 C rows,
6½" × 60½".

5 Join two taupe 1½" × 3" pieces, nine taupe 1½" × 5½" pieces, and 10 teal squares to make a sashing row measuring 1½" × 60½", including seam allowances. Make two of row D.

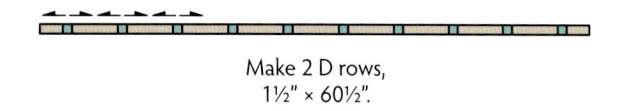

Make 2 D rows,
1½" × 60½".

6 Join two cream 1½" × 3" pieces, nine white 1½" × 5½" pieces, and 10 teal squares to make a sashing row measuring 1½" × 60½", including seam allowances. Make three of row E.

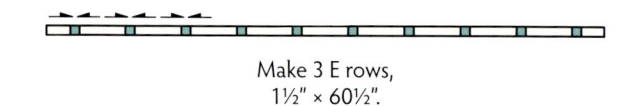

Make 3 E rows,
1½" × 60½".

7 Join the remaining taupe 1½"-wide strips end to end. From the pieced strip, cut eight 60½"-long strips.

8. Lay out rows A–E and the taupe strips as shown in the quilt assembly diagram below. Join the rows and strips. The quilt top should measure 60½" × 61½".

finishing the quilt

For more details on any finishing steps, visit ShopMartingale.com/HowtoQuilt for free downloadable information.

1. Layer the quilt top with batting and backing; baste the layers together.
2. Quilt by hand or machine. Robin's quilt is machine quilted with an allover leaf and swirl design.
3. Use the teal 2½"-wide strips to make double-fold binding and then attach the binding to the quilt.

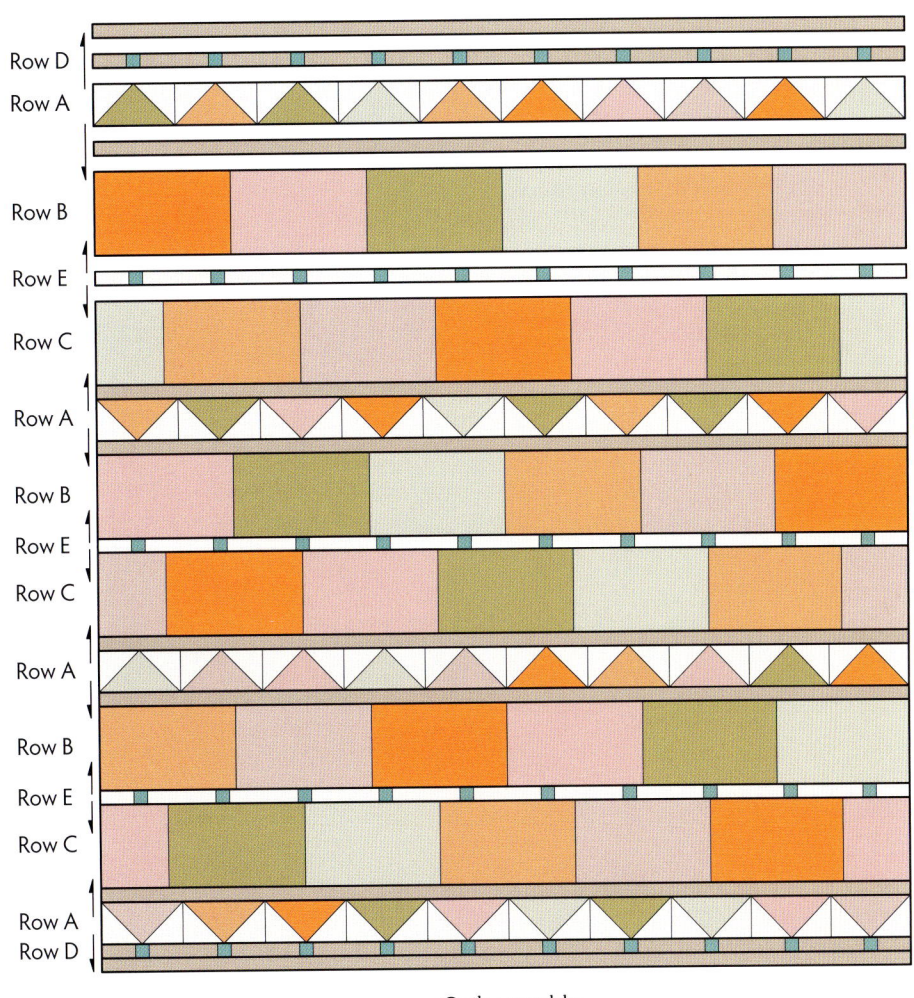

Quilt assembly

good fences, good neighbors

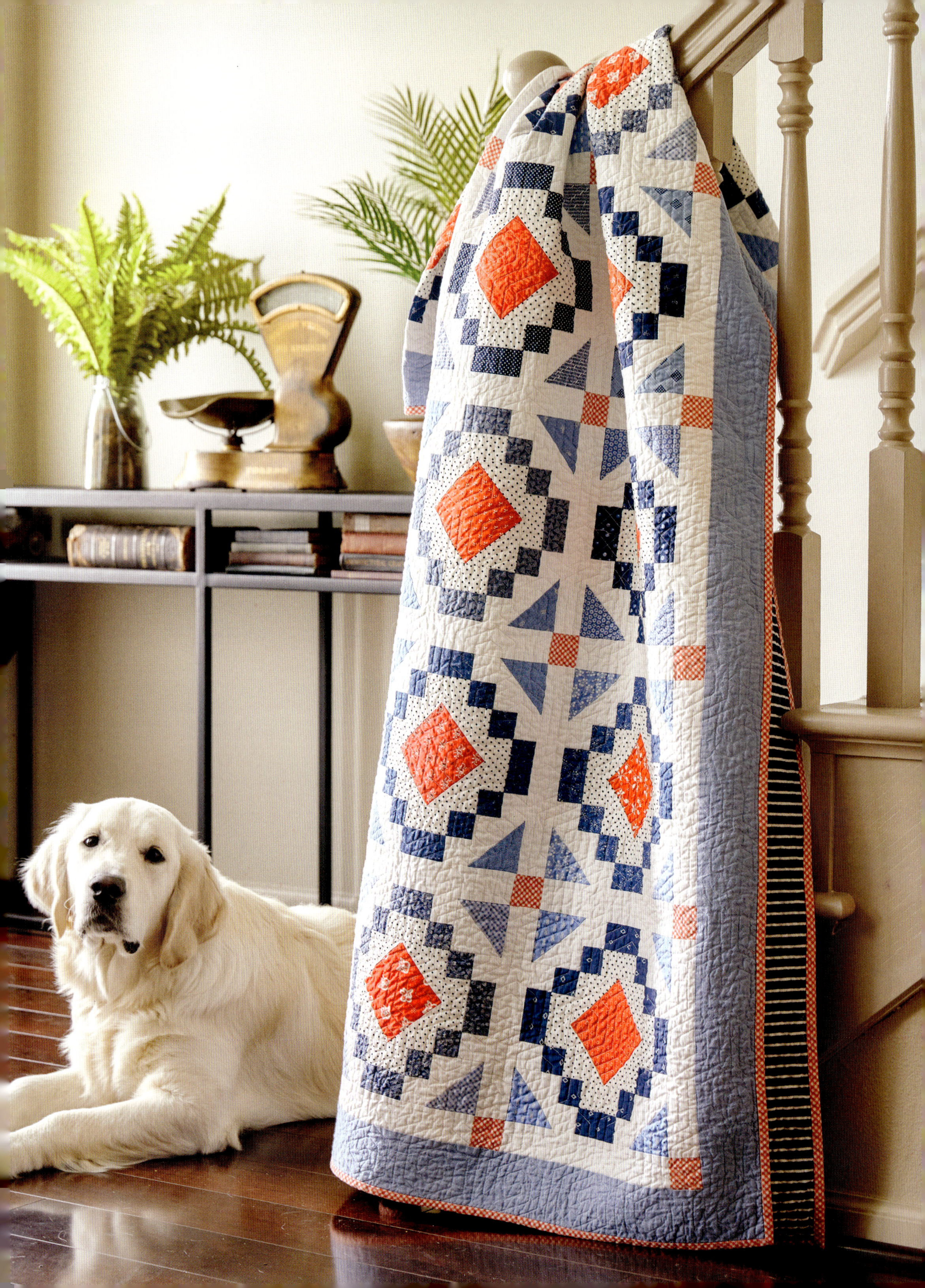

americana tiles

Like many quilters, Susan Ache is a big fan of red-white-and-blue quilts. With her scrappy mix of reds and both dark and light blues, each block looks like a decorative tile, and the blocks are all laid out with white grout, er, sashing.

Designed and pieced by Susan Ache; quilted by Susan Rogers

materials

Yardage is based on 42"-wide fabric. Fat quarters measure 18" × 21". Fat eighths measure 9" × 21". Susan used an assortment of fat quarters by Fig Tree & Co., Minick & Simpson, Crystal Manning, and others.

10 fat eighths of assorted medium blue prints (collectively referred to as "blue") for blocks

10 fat quarters of assorted dark blue and navy prints (collectively referred to as "navy") for blocks

¾ yard of blue print for border

10 fat eighths of assorted red prints for blocks

⅞ yard of red check for cornerstones and binding

2¾ yards of white solid for blocks and sashing

1½ yards of white dot for blocks

4⅝ yards of fabric for backing

71" × 83" piece of batting

cutting

All measurements include ¼" seam allowances. Keep like fabrics together.

From the white solid, cut:
- 4 strips, 10½" × 42"; crosscut into 71 strips, 2" × 10½"
- 6 strips, 3½" × 42"; crosscut into 60 squares, 3½" × 3½"
- 15 strips, 1¾" × 42"; crosscut into 30 strips, 1¾" × 15"

From *each* of the assorted blue prints, cut:
- 6 squares, 3½" × 3½" (60 total)

From *each* of the assorted navy prints, cut:
- 5 strips, 1¾" × 21"; crosscut into:
    3 strips, 1¾" × 15" (30 total)
    12 pieces, 1¾" × 3" (120 total)

From the white dot, cut:
- 10 strips, 3" × 42"; crosscut into 120 squares, 3" × 3"
- 10 strips, 1¾" × 42"; crosscut into 120 pieces, 1¾" × 3"

From *each* of the assorted red prints, cut:
- 3 squares, 5½" × 5½" (30 total)

From the red check, cut:
- 3 strips, 2" × 42"; crosscut into 42 squares, 2" × 2"
- 8 strips, 2½" × 42"

From the blue print for border, cut:
- 7 strips, 3½" × 42"

FINISHED QUILT:
65½" × 77"

FINISHED BLOCK:
10" × 10"

44 ♥ *snuggle up!*

making the blocks

Press seam allowances in the directions indicated by the arrows. In steps 1–3, keep like units or segments together.

1 Draw a diagonal line from corner to corner on the wrong side of the white solid 3½" squares. Layer a marked square on a blue print square, right sides together. Sew ¼" from both sides of the drawn line. Cut the unit apart on the marked line to make two half-square-triangle units. Trim the units to 3" square, including seam allowances. Make 120 units.

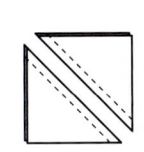

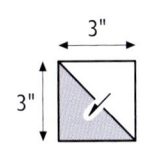

Make 120 units.

2 Sew a white solid 1¾" × 15" strip to the long side of a navy strip to make a strip set measuring 3" × 15", including seam allowances. Make a total of 30 strip sets. Cut each strip set into eight segments, 1¾" × 3" (240 total).

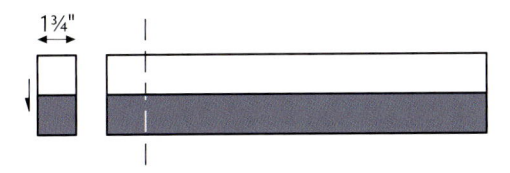

Make 30 strip sets, 3" × 15".
Cut 240 segments, 1¾" × 3".

3 Using one navy print throughout this step, join white dot and navy 1¾" × 3" pieces along their long edges. Sew a segment from step 2 to each end to make a side unit. Make 120 units measuring 3" × 5½", including seam allowances.

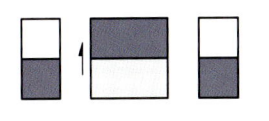

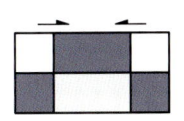

Make 120 units, 3" × 5½".

4 Draw a diagonal line from corner to corner on the wrong side of the white dot 3" squares. Place marked squares on opposite corners of a red print 5½" square. Sew on the marked line. Trim the excess corner fabric ¼" from the stitched line. Place marked squares on the

getting cozy with Susan Ache

If there's a chill in the air, I'm sure to have some sort of vegetable casserole in the oven.

When I'm ready to snuggle up with a quilt, I also need the remote control and my stitching in my lap.

If I were the chancellor of Cozy College, my school uniform would be "lounge clothes," which is one step above pajamas. Baggy sweats and a T-shirt round out my home attire.

Batting is the unseen hero in making a quilt cozy. Here's my choice for a quilt you can wrap up with: one that is super soft and drapes like an antique quilt does after about 100 washings.

If there's a bowl of popcorn and my favorite beverage, I'm having only Pop Secret Homestyle butter popcorn with diet Dr. Pepper.

When I'm curled under a quilt, the fabric backing is often just as visible to me as the top. So here's my tip for choosing backing fabric: For tablecloths, I love a wide-backing fabric so I can flip it over for another look entirely. If it's for a bed or lap, then it's scrappy all the way with leftover fabrics from the front.

For me, a quilt to curl up with has to at least go from the top of my toes all the way up to my lap where it bunches.

My happy place to snuggle up with a quilt is wherever I am! My quilts just have to be within reach. Everybody in the family has their favorites that are also within their reach.

Color has a vibe for many people. Other than the color combination I used in this book, a color combination that says "cozy" to me is any shade of orange with any other color. But, I make red-and-white quilts because they're so pretty folded and stacked around the house.

Instagram: @yardgrl60

remaining corners of the square. Sew and trim as before to make a center unit measuring 5½" square, including seam allowances. Make 30 units.

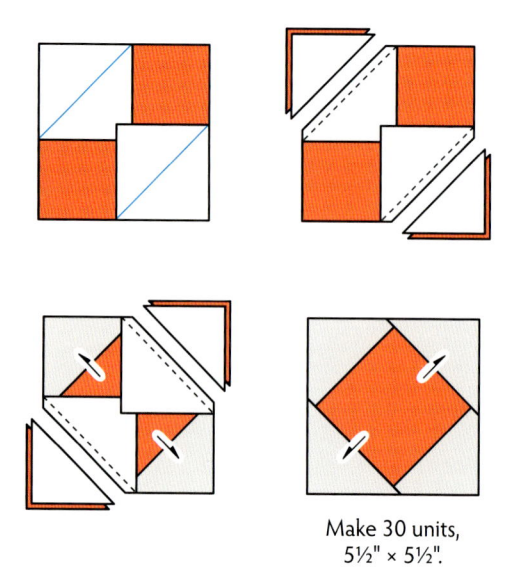

Make 30 units, 5½" × 5½".

5 Lay out four matching half-square-triangle units, four matching side units, and one center unit in three rows as shown. Sew the units into rows. Join the rows to make a block measuring 10½" square, including seam allowances. Make 30 blocks.

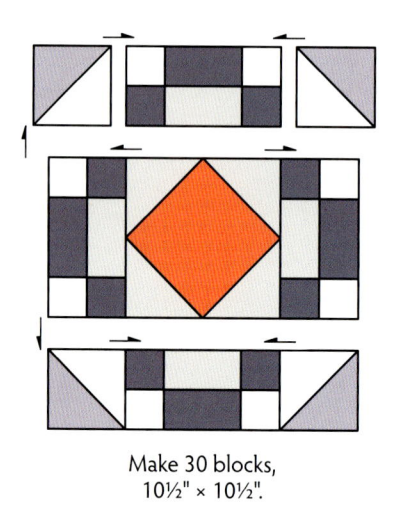

Make 30 blocks, 10½" × 10½".

assembling the quilt top

1 Join five white solid 2" × 10½" strips and six red check squares to make a sashing row measuring 2" × 59½", including seam allowances. Make seven rows.

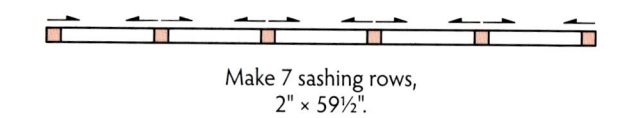

Make 7 sashing rows, 2" × 59½".

2 Join five blocks and six white solid 2" × 10½" strips to make a block row measuring 10½" × 59½", including seam allowances. Make six rows.

Make 6 block rows,
10½" × 59½".

3 Join the block rows and sashing rows, alternating the positions as shown in the quilt assembly diagram below. The quilt top should measure 59½" × 71", including seam allowances.

4 Join the blue 3½"-wide strips end to end. From the pieced strip, cut two 71"-long strips and two 65½"-long strips. Sew the longer strips to the left and right sides of the quilt center. Sew the shorter strips to the top and bottom edges. The quilt top should measure 65½" × 77".

finishing the quilt

For more details on any finishing steps, visit ShopMartingale.com/HowtoQuilt for free downloadable information.

1 Layer the quilt top with batting and backing; baste the layers together.

2 Quilt by hand or machine. Susan's quilt is machine quilted with an allover design of large swirls.

3 Use the red check 2½"-wide strips to make binding and then attach the binding to the quilt.

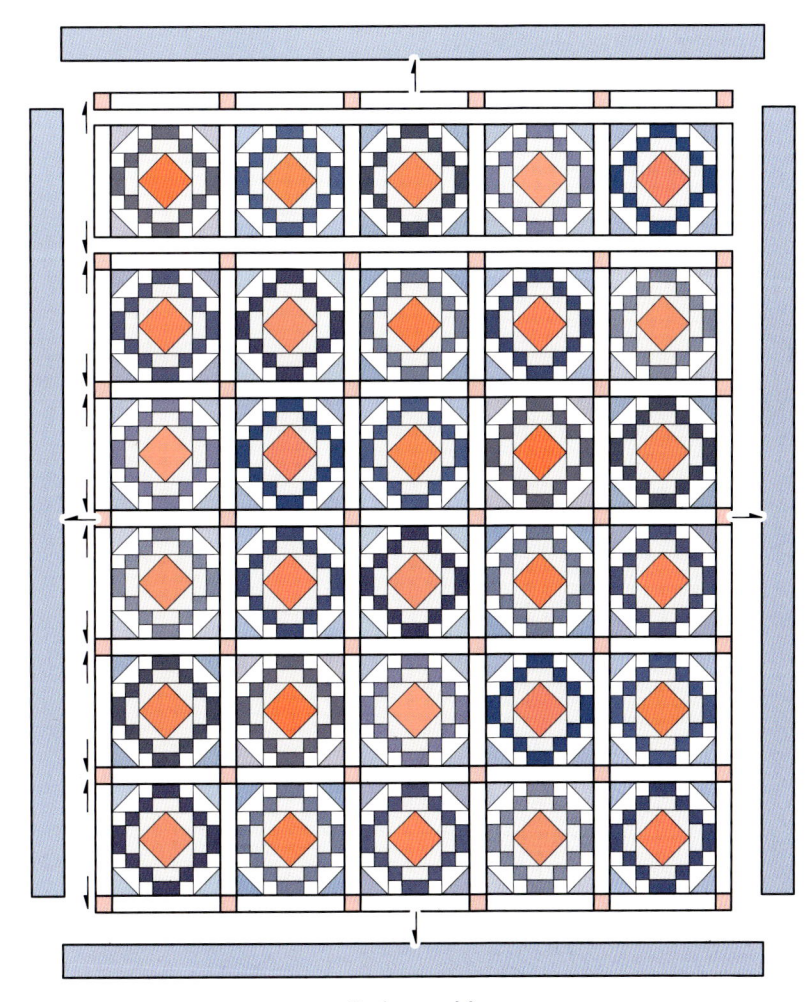

Quilt assembly

americana tiles

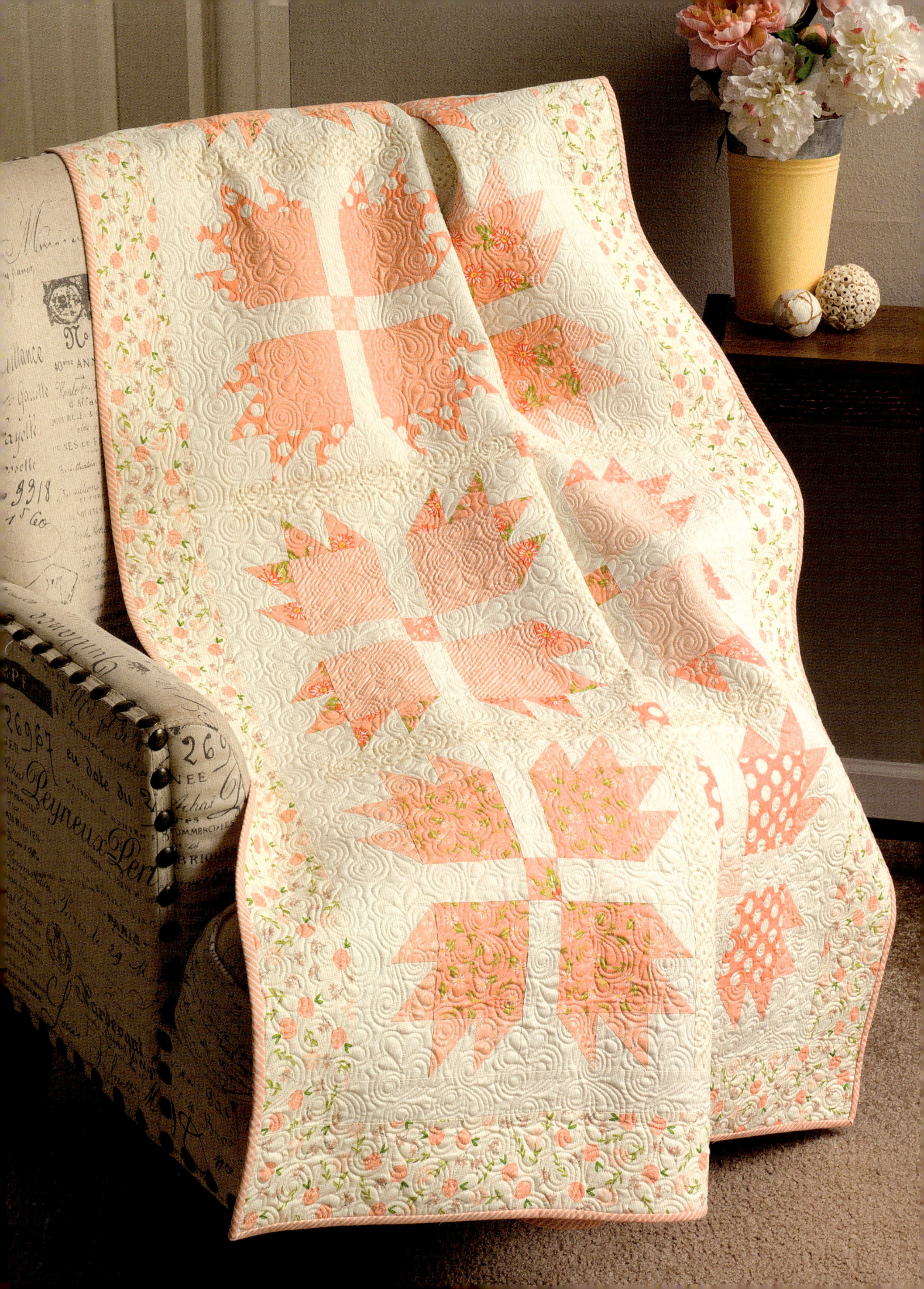

coral garden

Designer Sherri McConnell takes a time-honored block, Bear's Paw, and turns it into a soft and romantic Coral Garden quilt, perfect to snuggle under in your favorite reading spot. But it's OK if under this dreamy quilt you fall asleep partway through the chapter. No one will blame you!

Designed and pieced by Sherri L. McConnell; quilted by Marion Bott

materials

Yardage is based on 42"-wide fabric. Fat quarters measure 18" × 21". Sherri used fabrics from Sincerely Yours, Happy Days, Balboa, Summer Sweet, and Front Porch, all by Sherri & Chelsi for Moda Fabrics.

2 yards of cream solid for blocks and inner border

12 fat quarters of assorted coral prints for blocks and cornerstones

⅝ yard of light print for sashing

¾ yard of coral floral for outer border

⅝ yard of coral diagonal stripe for binding

3½ yards of fabric for backing

60" × 75" piece of batting

cutting

All measurements include ¼" seam allowances.

From the cream solid, cut:
- 8 strips, 3" × 42"; crosscut into 96 squares, 3" × 3"
- 3 strips, 2½" × 42"; crosscut into 48 squares, 2½" × 2½"
- 14 strips, 2" × 42"; crosscut *8 of the strips* into 48 strips, 2" × 6½"

From *each* of the assorted coral prints, cut:
- 4 squares, 4½" × 4½" (48 total)
- 8 squares, 3" × 3" (96 total)
- 2 squares, 2" × 2" (24 total; 6 are extra)

From the light print, cut:
- 9 strips, 2" × 42"; crosscut into 17 strips, 2" × 14"

From the coral floral, cut:
- 6 strips, 4" × 42"

From the coral diagonal stripe, cut:
- 7 strips, 2½" × 42"

TRIANGLE PAPER

Using triangle papers to make the half-square-triangle units can save a lot of time. Instead of cutting cream and coral 3" squares, follow the manufacturer's instructions for your favorite triangle paper to make 12 sets of 16 matching units. If you choose this method, skip step 1 of "Making the Blocks" on page 51.

FINISHED QUILT:
54" × 69"
FINISHED BLOCK:
13½" × 13½"

50 ♥ snuggle up!

making the blocks

Press seam allowances in the directions indicated by the arrows.

1 Draw a diagonal line from corner to corner on the wrong side of the cream 3" squares. Layer a marked square on a coral print 3" square, right sides together. Sew ¼" from both sides of the drawn line. Cut the unit apart on the marked line to make two half-square-triangle units. Trim the units to 2½" square, including seam allowances. Make 12 sets of 16 matching units.

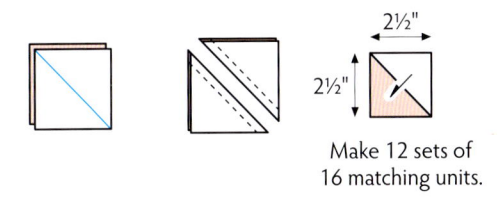

Make 12 sets of 16 matching units.

2 Lay out four matching half-square-triangle units, one cream 2½" square, and one coral print 4½" square from a different print in two rows. Sew the units and squares into rows. Join the rows to make a corner unit measuring 6½" square, including seam allowances. Make 12 sets of four matching units.

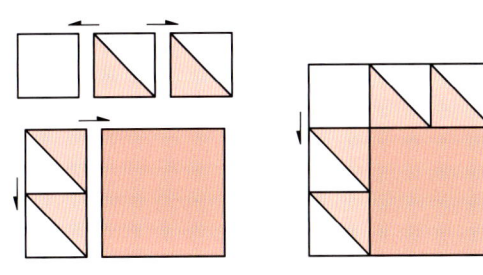

Make 12 sets of 4 matching units, 6½" × 6½".

getting cozy with Sherri McConnell

If there's a chill in the air, I'm sure to have soup in the slow cooker.

When I'm ready to snuggle up with a quilt, I also need a book.

If I were the chancellor of Cozy College, my school uniform would be comfy jeans or shorts and a T-shirt.

Batting is the unseen hero in making a quilt cozy. Here's my choice for a quilt you can wrap up with: Hobbs Warm & White.

If there's a bowl of popcorn and my favorite beverage, I'm having plain popcorn. (Chicago Mix is good too, but so addicting.) I love lemonade with a splash of mango nectar or strawberry slush—fruity drinks are my favorites!

When I'm curled under a quilt, the fabric backing is often just as visible to me as the top. So here's my tip for choosing backing fabric: I always choose favorite prints for backings.

For me, a quilt to curl up with has to at least cover my lap, except when it actually gets cold where I live! Then it has to cover more.

My happy place to snuggle up with a quilt is my family room when watching TV. Often the quilt on my lap is one I'm binding. I do love hand binding!

Color has a vibe for many people. Other than the color combination I used in this book, a color combination that says "cozy" to me is a great mix of blues and low-volume prints.

AQuiltingLife.com

3. Lay out four matching corner units, four cream 2" × 6½" strips, and one coral print 2" square in three rows. Sew into rows and then join the rows to make a block. Make 12 blocks measuring 14" square, including seam allowances.

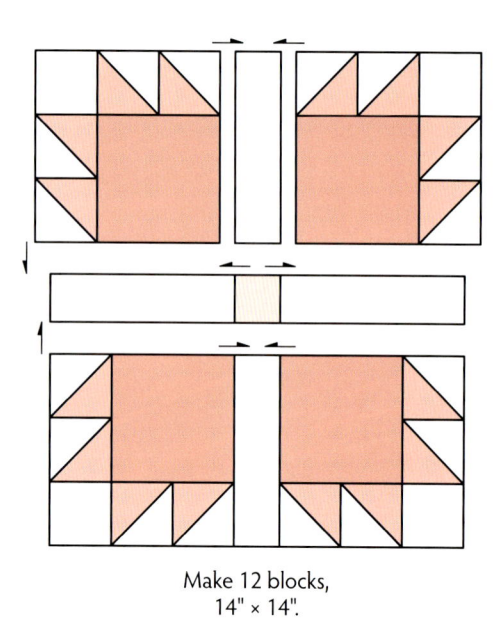

Make 12 blocks, 14" × 14".

assembling the quilt top

1. Join three blocks and two light strips to make a block row measuring 14" × 44", including seam allowances. Make four rows.

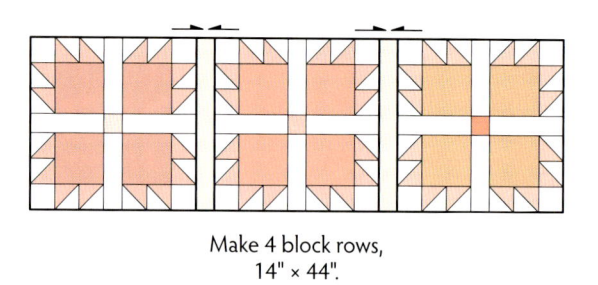

Make 4 block rows, 14" × 44".

2. Join three light strips and two coral print 2" squares to make a sashing row measuring 2" × 44", including seam allowances. Make three rows.

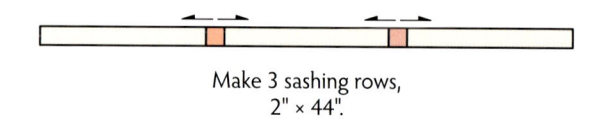

Make 3 sashing rows, 2" × 44".

3 Join the block rows and sashing rows, alternating them as shown in the quilt assembly diagram below. The quilt top should measure 44" × 59", including seam allowances.

4 Join the remaining cream 2"-wide strips end to end. From the pieced strip, cut two 59"-long strips and two 47"-long strips. Sew the longer strips to the left and right sides of the quilt center. Sew the shorter strips to the top and bottom edges. The quilt top should measure 47" × 62", including seam allowances.

5 Join the coral floral 4"-wide strips end to end. From the pieced strip, cut two 62"-long strips and two 54"-long strips. Sew the longer strips to opposite sides of the quilt center. Sew the shorter strips to the top and bottom edges. The quilt top should measure 54" × 69".

finishing the quilt

For more details on any finishing steps, visit ShopMartingale.com/HowtoQuilt for free downloadable information.

1 Layer the quilt top with batting and backing; baste the layers together.

2 Quilt by hand or machine. Sherri's quilt is machine quilted with an allover swirl design.

3 Use the coral stripe 2½"-wide strips to make double-fold binding and then attach the binding to the quilt.

Quilt assembly

coral garden 53

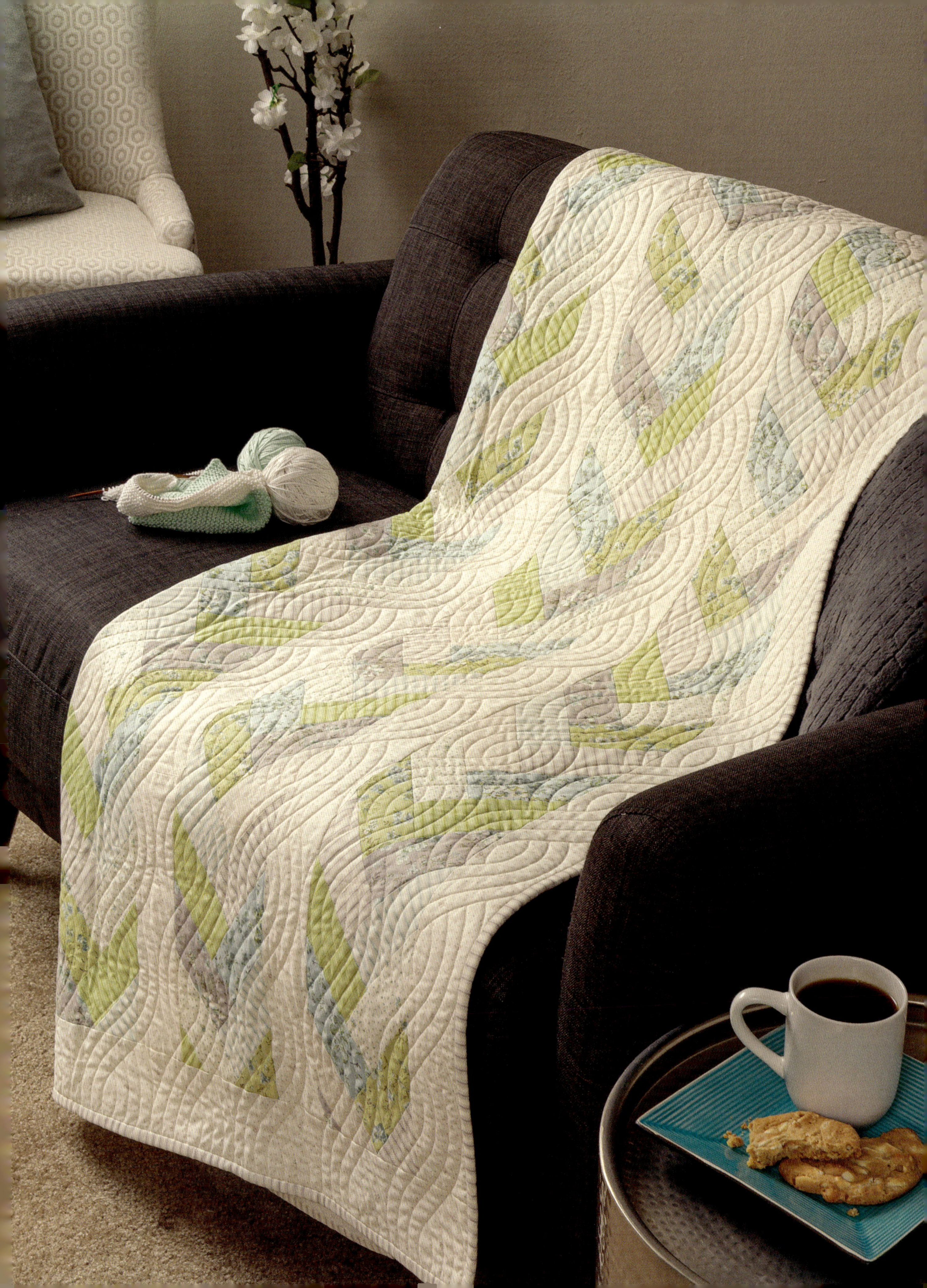

woven together

The classic chevrons in this design from Brenda Riddle are surprisingly easy to sew—much easier than they look. Here, she has woven together a soft palette of blues, greens, and grays in a design that will bring a note of sophistication to any decor.

Designed and pieced by Brenda Riddle; quilted by Nicole Christoffersen

materials

Yardage is based on 42"-wide fabric. Brenda used Dover by Brenda Riddle Designs for Moda Fabrics.

½ yard *each* of 8 assorted prints for braid columns

1½ yards of cream print for sashing and border

⅝ yard of gray stripe for binding

3¼ yards of fabric for backing

57" × 80" piece of batting

cutting

All measurements include ¼" seam allowances.

From *each* of the assorted prints, cut:
- 6 strips, 2½" × 42"; crosscut into:
    32 strips, 2½" × 6" (256 total; 6 are extra)
    1 square, 2½" × 2½" (8 total; 3 are extra)

From the cream print, cut:
- 13 strips, 3½" × 42"

From the gray stripe, cut:
- 7 strips, 2½" × 42"

assembling the quilt top

Press seam allowances in the directions indicated by the arrows.

1. Sew a print strip to the top edge of a print square. Sew a different print strip to the right edge of the unit.

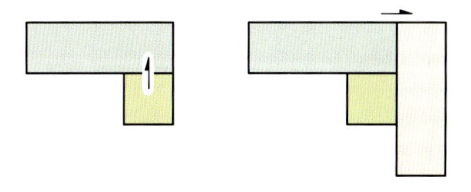

2. Sew print strips to the top and then right edges of the unit from step 1.

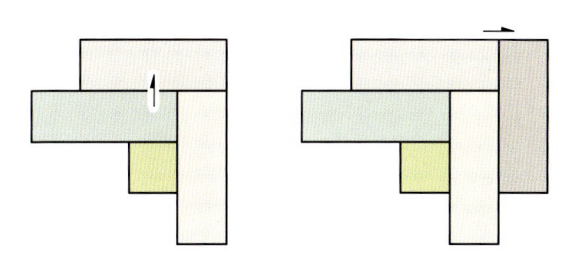

FINISHED QUILT:
51" × 74"

56 ♥ snuggle up!

3 Continue sewing strips to the upper-left and upper-right edges until you have 25 strips on each side. Press all seam allowances toward each newly added strip. Make five columns.

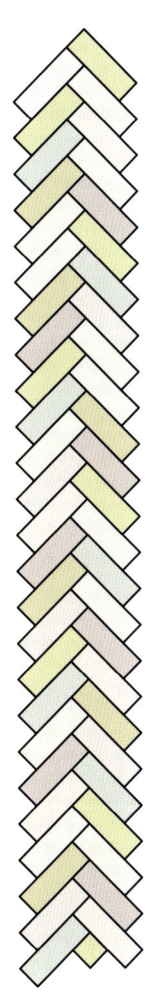

Make 5 columns.

MIX IT UP!

If you find yourself stressing over which strip to add next for a scrappy look, try this: Put all the 2½" × 6" pieces in a paper bag and shake the bag to toss them around. Without looking, pull a strip out of the bag and sew it to your growing column. Continue pulling pieces randomly and adding them in the order you select them.

getting cozy with
Brenda Riddle

If there's a chill in the air, I'm sure to have soup on the stove.

When I'm ready to snuggle up with a quilt, I also need my pup Emmie.

If I were the chancellor of Cozy College, my school uniform would be definitely knit tops and bottoms.

Batting is the unseen hero in making a quilt cozy. Here's my choice for a quilt you can wrap up with: Quilters Dream Cotton, Request Loft.

If there's a bowl of popcorn and my favorite beverage, I'm having popcorn with chili-lime seasoning and a sparkling water.

When I'm curled under a quilt, the fabric backing is often just as visible to me as the top. So here's my tip for choosing backing fabric: I love using both sides of a quilt, so I always coordinate the binding to work with both the front and back.

For me, a quilt to curl up with has to at least go from my shoulders to cover my toes (just in case I want to snooze under it too).

My happy place to snuggle up with a quilt is my oversized chair.

Color has a vibe for many people. Other than the color combination I used in this book, a color combination that says "cozy" to me is any faded soft colors and a lighter background.

BrendaRiddleDesigns.com

woven together 57

4 On the long side of each column, align a ruler with the inside point of the seam intersection, placing the ruler's 45° line on a seamline. Trim along the edge of the ruler, moving it down the length of the column. Repeat to trim the other side of the column. Trim the bottom edge in the same way. Measure 68" from the trimmed bottom edge and trim the top edge. The columns should each measure 7" × 68", including seam allowances.

7"

68"

Make 5 columns, 7" × 68".

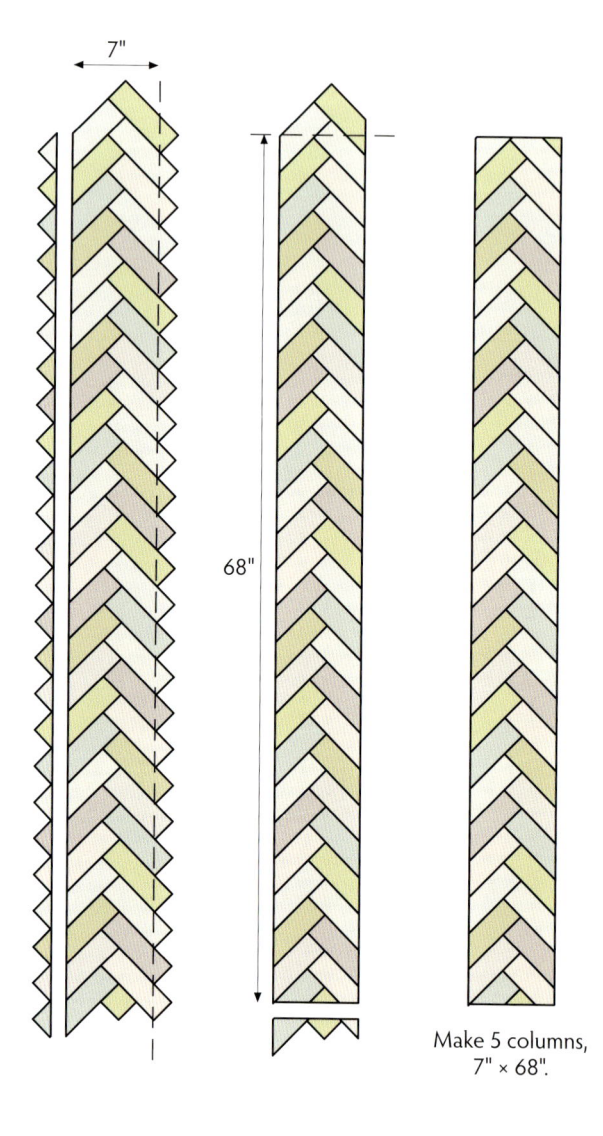

5. Join the cream 3½"-wide strips end to end. From the pieced strip, cut six 68"-long strips and two 51"-long strips.

6. Referring to the quilt assembly diagram, join the braid columns and cream 68"-long strips, alternating them as shown. Notice how the braided columns have been rotated so the chevrons point downward, rather than upward as they were sewn. If you prefer, your chevrons can point upward! Sew the cream 51"-long strips to the top and bottom edges. The quilt top should measure 51" × 74".

finishing the quilt

For more details on any finishing steps, visit ShopMartingale.com/HowtoQuilt for free downloadable information.

1. Layer the quilt top with batting and backing; baste the layers together.

2. Quilt by hand or machine. Brenda's quilt is machine quilted with side-by-side vertical cable patterns.

3. Use the gray stripe 2½"-wide strips to make double-fold binding and then attach the binding to the quilt.

Quilt assembly

woven together 59

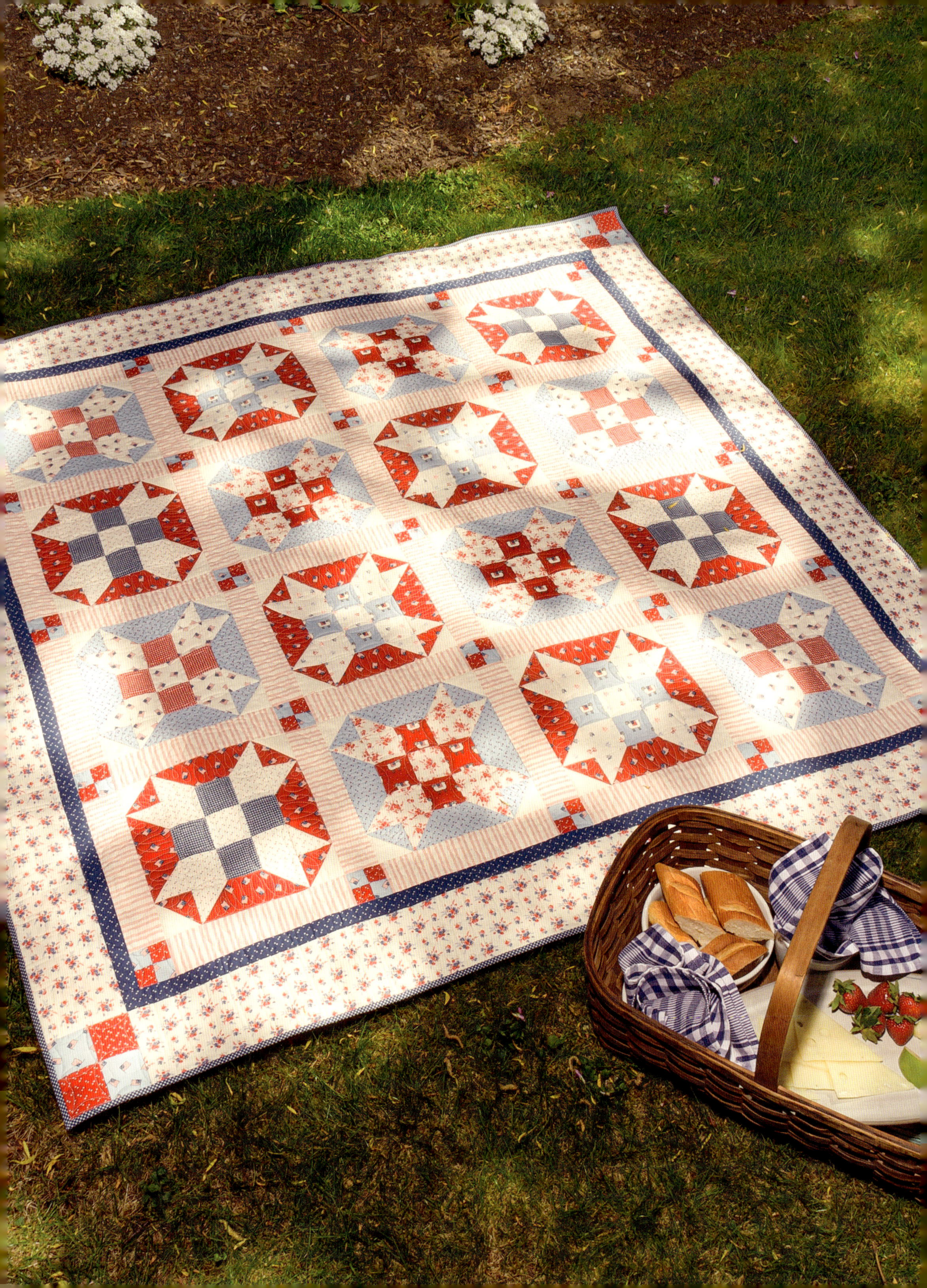

summer picnic

Look closely and you'll see that Anne Sutton's patriotic fabrics include flags on poles as well as some little sheep wearing flags. These adorable prints mingle with dainty florals and whimsical checks and stripes, creating a perfect mix for a summertime picnic or to use on a porch swing.

Designed by Anne Sutton, pieced by Nancy Ritter, and quilted by Rebecca Hubel

materials

Yardage is based on 42"-wide fabric. Anne used Prairie Days by Bunny Hill Designs for Moda Fabrics.

⅝ yard *each* of red A and blue A prints for blocks

⅜ yard *each* of 4 assorted cream prints for blocks

⅛ yard *each* of 2 red B and 2 blue B prints for block centers

¼ yard *each* of red C and blue C prints for four-patch units

⅓ yard of white solid for blocks

1⅛ yards of cream-and-red stripe for sashing

⅓ yard of navy print for inner border

⅞ yard of cream floral for outer border

⅝ yard of navy check for binding

3¾ yards of fabric for backing

67" × 67" square of batting

cutting

All measurements include ¼" seam allowances. Cut the A and B strips carefully; you will not have any leftover fabric.

From the white solid, cut:
- 3 strips, 2⅞" × 42"; crosscut into 32 squares, 2⅞" × 2⅞"

From *each* of the A prints, cut:
- 2 strips, 6½" × 42"; crosscut into 32 strips, 2½" × 6½" (64 total)
- 2 strips, 2⅞" × 42"; crosscut into 16 squares, 2⅞" × 2⅞" (32 total)

From *each* of the cream prints, cut:
- 4 strips, 2½" × 42"; crosscut into 52 squares, 2½" × 2½" (208 total)

From *each* of the B prints, cut:
- 1 strip, 2½" × 42"; crosscut into 16 squares, 2½" × 2½" (64 total)

From *each* of the C prints, cut:
- 1 strip, 2½" × 42"; crosscut into 8 squares, 2½" × 2½" (16 total)
- 2 strips, 1½" × 42" (4 total)

From the cream-and-red stripe, cut:
- 14 strips, 2½" × 42"; crosscut into 40 strips, 2½" × 10½"

From the navy print, cut:
- 6 strips, 1½" × 42"

From the cream floral, cut:
- 6 strips, 4½" × 42"

From the navy check, cut:
- 7 strips, 2½" × 42"

FINISHED QUILT:
60½" × 60½"
FINISHED BLOCK:
10" × 10"

making the blocks

Refer to the photo above for fabric placement guidance throughout. Press seam allowances in the directions indicated by the arrows.

1. Draw a diagonal line from corner to corner on the wrong side of the white 2⅞" squares. Layer a marked square on a red A or blue A 2⅞" square, right sides together. Sew ¼" from both sides of the drawn line. Cut the unit apart on the marked line to make two half-square-triangle units measuring 2½" square, including seam allowances. Make 32 red A and 32 blue A units.

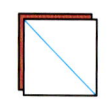

Make 32 of each unit, 2½" × 2½".

62 ♥ *snuggle up!*

2 Draw a diagonal line from corner to corner on the wrong side of 128 of the cream print 2½" squares. Place a marked square on one end of a red A strip, right sides together. Sew on the marked line. Trim the excess corner fabric ¼" from the stitched line. Place a matching square on the opposite end of the red strip. Sew and trim as before to make a side unit measuring 2½" × 6½", including seam allowances. Make two sets of 16 matching red units (32 total).

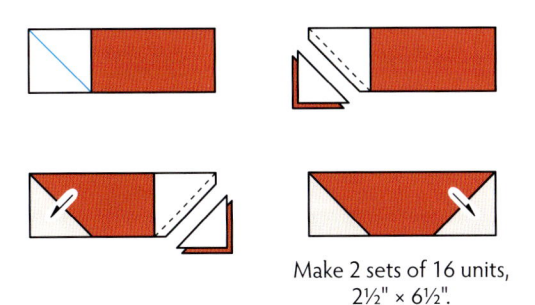

Make 2 sets of 16 units, 2½" × 6½".

3 Repeat step 2 using the remaining marked cream squares and the blue A strips to make two sets of 16 matching blue side units (32 total). The units should measure 2½" × 6½", including seam allowances.

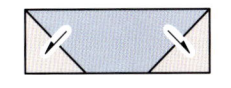

Make 2 sets of 16 units, 2½" × 6½".

4 Using cream print squares that match those used for the red side units, lay out five matching cream print 2½" squares and four matching blue B squares in three rows of three. Sew the squares into rows. Join the rows to make a nine-patch unit measuring 6½" square, including seam allowances. Make two sets of four matching blue units.

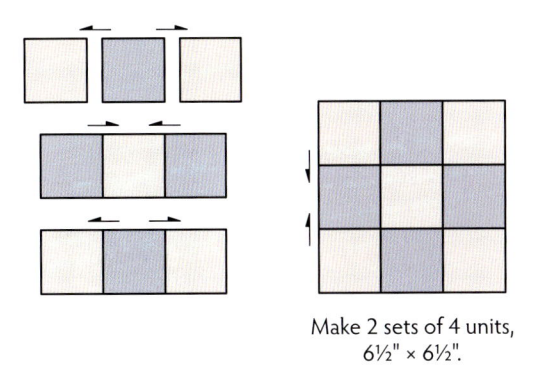

Make 2 sets of 4 units, 6½" × 6½".

5 Lay out five matching cream print 2½" squares and four matching red B squares in three rows of three. Sew the squares into rows. Join the rows to make a nine-patch unit measuring 6½" square, including seam allowances. Make two sets of four matching red units.

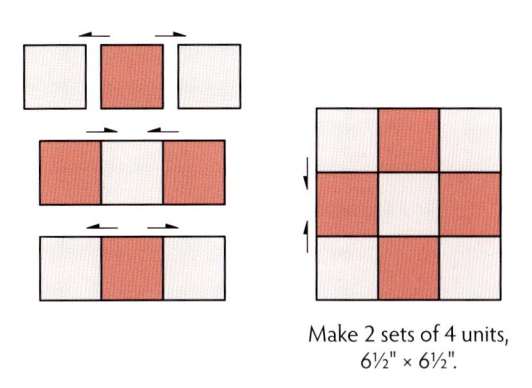

Make 2 sets of 4 units, 6½" × 6½".

6 Lay out four red half-square-triangle units, four red side units, and one blue nine-patch unit in three rows. The red and cream prints should be the same throughout. Sew the units into rows. Join the rows to make a red block measuring 10½" square, including seam allowances. Make eight blocks.

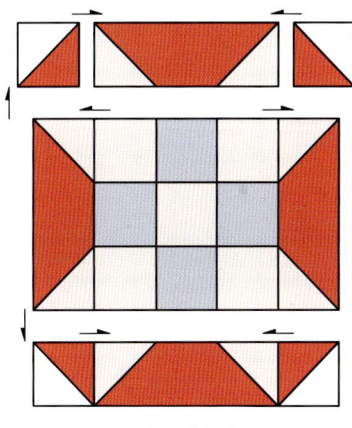

Make 8 blocks, 10½" × 10½".

summer picnic ♥ 63

7 Lay out four blue half-square-triangle units, four blue side units, and one red nine-patch unit in three rows. The blue and cream prints should be the same throughout. Sew the units into rows. Join the rows to make a blue block measuring 10½" square, including seam allowances. Make eight blocks.

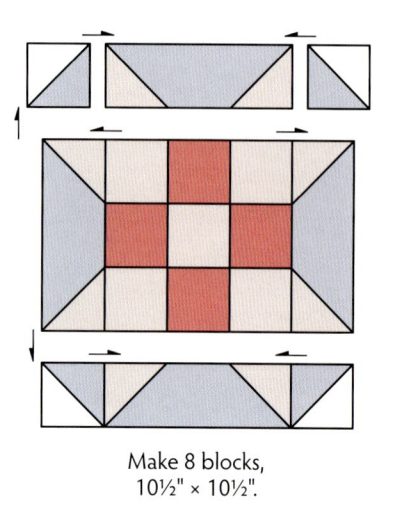

Make 8 blocks,
10½" × 10½".

assembling the quilt top

1 Join one red C and one blue C 1½" × 42" strip to make a strip set measuring 2½" × 42", including seam allowances. Make two. Cut the strip sets into 50 segments, 1½" × 2½".

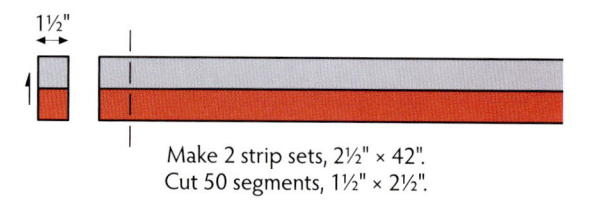

Make 2 strip sets, 2½" × 42".
Cut 50 segments, 1½" × 2½".

2 Join two segments from step 1 to make a four-patch unit measuring 2½" square, including seam allowances. Make 25 units.

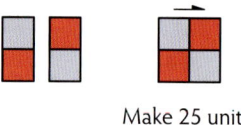

Make 25 units,
2½" × 2½".

3 Join five four-patch units and four cream-and-red stripe strips to make a sashing row. Make five rows measuring 2½" × 50½", including seam allowances.

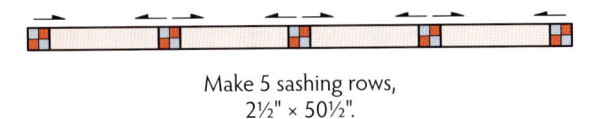

Make 5 sashing rows, 2½" × 50½".

4 Join five cream-and-red stripe strips, two different blue blocks, and two different red blocks to make a block row. Notice that the blue and red blocks alternate. Make four rows measuring 10½" × 50½", including seam allowances.

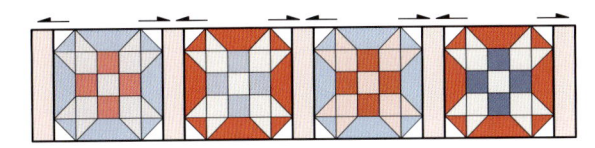

Make 4 block rows, 10½" × 50½".

5 Referring to the quilt assembly diagram on page 66, join the sashing rows and block rows, rotating every other block row so that blue and red blocks are always next to one another. The quilt top should measure 50½" square, including seam allowances.

adding the borders

1 Join the navy print 1½"-wide strips end to end. From the pieced strip, cut two 52½"-long strips and two 50½"-long strips. Sew the shorter strips to the left and right sides of the quilt center. Sew the longer strips to the top and bottom edges. The quilt top should measure 52½" square, including seam allowances.

2 Lay out two red C and two blue C 2½" squares in two rows of two. Sew the squares into rows. Join the rows to make a four-patch unit measuring 4½" square, including seam allowances. Make four units.

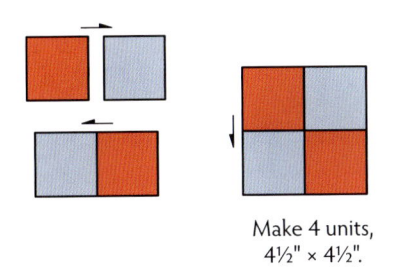

Make 4 units, 4½" × 4½".

getting cozy with Anne Sutton

When I'm ready to snuggle up with a quilt, I'm sure to have a good book to read on my iPad.

If I were the chancellor of Cozy College, my school uniform would be sweats.

Batting is the unseen hero in making a quilt cozy. Here's my choice for a quilt you can wrap up with: Quilters Dream Cotton, Request Loft.

If there's a bowl of popcorn and my favorite beverage, I prefer a fresh-baked pretzel and a glass of Clausthaler beer.

When I'm curled under a quilt, the fabric backing is often just as visible to me as the top. So here's my tip for choosing backing fabric: I love being able to see the quilting on the back, so I like to choose a tiny print with lots of spacing.

For me, a quilt to curl up with has to at least tuck around my toes and then cover my shoulders too.

My happy place to snuggle up with a quilt is on the daybed in our family room.

Color has a vibe for many people. Other than the color combination I used in this book, a color combination that says "cozy" to me is shades of pink and taupe.

BunnyHillDesigns.com

summer picnic ♥ 65

3 Join the cream floral 4½"-wide strips end to end. From the pieced strip, cut four 52½"-long strips. Sew two strips to opposite sides of the quilt center.

4 Sew a four-patch unit to each end of the remaining cream floral strips from step 3. Sew the strips to the top and bottom edges of the quilt top. The quilt top should measure 60½" square.

finishing the quilt

For more details on any finishing steps, visit ShopMartingale.com/HowtoQuilt for free downloadable information.

1 Layer the quilt top with batting and backing; baste the layers together.

2 Quilt by hand or machine. Anne's quilt is machine quilted with curved lines and loops in the blocks. Ribbon candy is stitched in the sashing and curved lines are stitched in the four patches. Parallel straight lines are stitched in the outer border.

3 Use the navy check 2½"-wide strips to make double-fold binding, then attach the binding to the quilt.

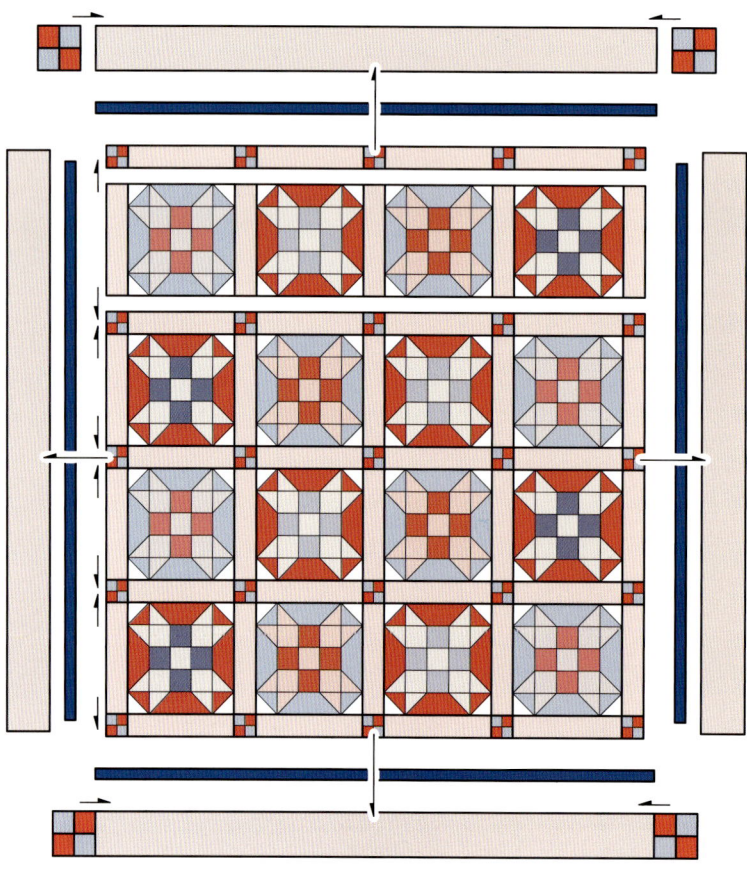

Quilt assembly

66 ♥ snuggle up!

rustic retreat

You don't need to live in a log cabin or rustic farmhouse to appreciate the snuggly goodness of Lisa Bongean's design. Brushed cottons in monochromatic grays, blacks, and browns are sure to bring enjoyment anywhere, including on a modern leather couch!

Designed and pieced by Lisa Bongean; quilted by Luke Neubauer and Jake Neubauer

materials

Yardage is based on 42"-wide fabric. Fat quarters measure 18" × 21". Lisa used Urban Homestead by Primitive Gatherings for Moda Fabrics.

20 fat quarters of assorted plaids and stripes in cream, black, gray, and brown for blocks and star units*

2⅜ yards of light gray crossweave fabric for sashing and border

⅝ yard of gray plaid for binding

4½ yards of fabric for backing

64" × 81" piece of batting

2" finished Triangle Papers from Primitive Gatherings (optional)

*Lisa used 5 cream, 5 black, 5 gray, and 5 brown plaids and stripes.

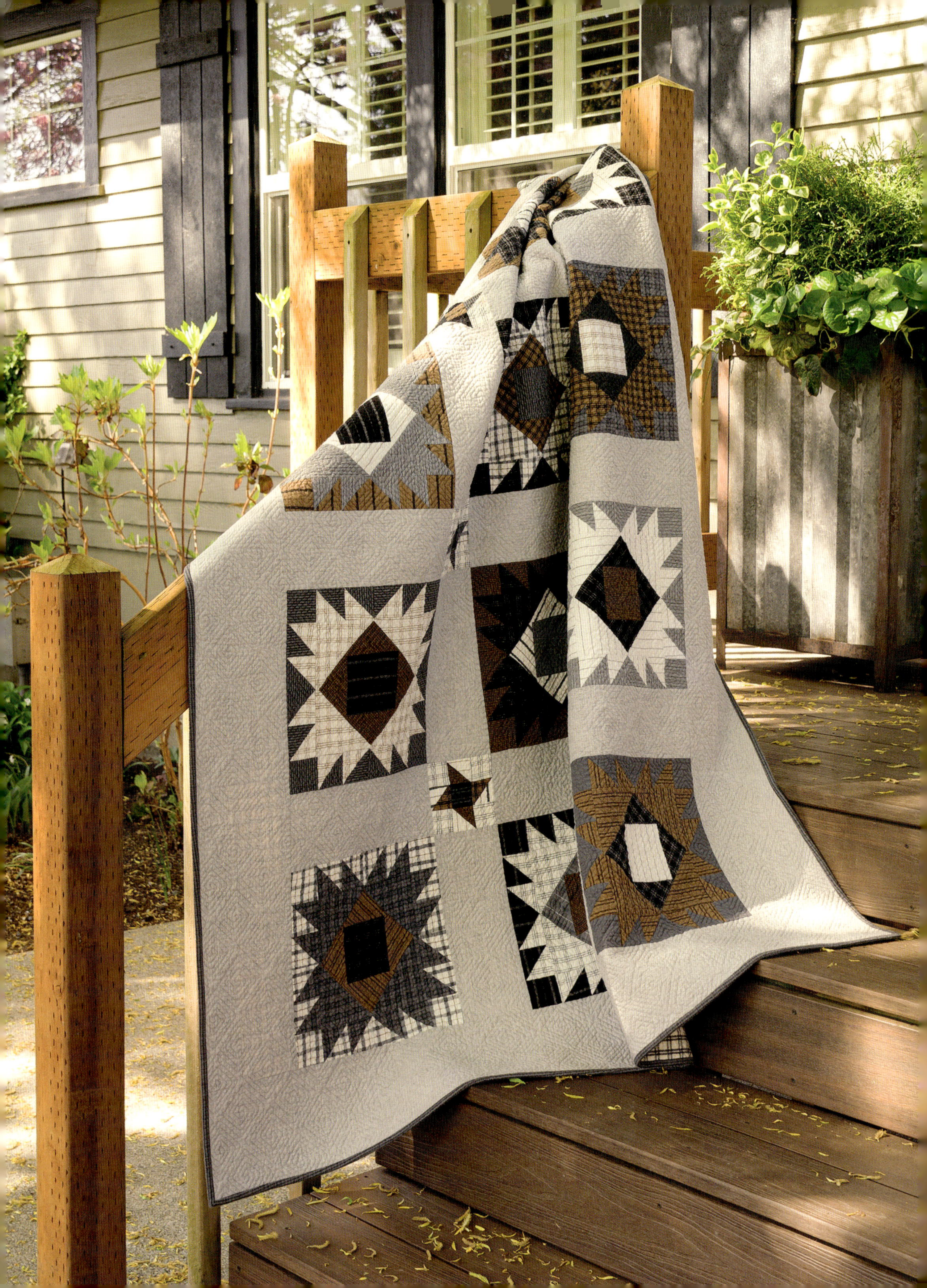

cutting

Cutting is given for 1 block at a time; the number of pieces listed in parentheses provides the total amount needed to make 12 blocks. So, before you begin cutting, choose 1 cream, 1 black, 1 gray, and 1 brown fabric and label them fabrics A–D. Keep in mind that you'll use the same fabric in more than 1 block, but the fabric's position may be different from block to block (the same fabric may be A in the first block and B in the next). Refer to the quilt photo on page 70 for fabric placement guidance. For greater ease in piecing, keep the pieces for each block grouped together. All measurements include ¼" seam allowances.

CUTTING FOR 1 BLOCK

Repeat to make 12 blocks.

From fabric A, cut:
- 4 squares, 2½" × 2½" (48 total)

If using Triangle Papers, cut:
- 1 square, 10" × 10" (12 total)

If not using Triangle Papers, cut:
- 8 squares, 2⅞" × 2⅞" (96 total)

From fabric B, cut:
- 2 squares, 5½" × 5½"; cut the squares in half diagonally to yield 4 triangles (48 total)

If using Triangle Papers, cut:
- 1 square, 10" × 10" (12 total)

If not using Triangle Papers, cut:
- 8 squares, 2⅞" × 2⅞" (96 total)

From fabric C, cut:
- 2 squares, 4¼" × 4¼"; cut the squares in half diagonally to yield 4 triangles (48 total)

From fabric D, cut:
- 1 square, 4¼" × 4¼" (12 total)

ADDITIONAL CUTTING TO COMPLETE THE QUILT

From 1 of the cream plaids, cut:
- 24 squares, 2" × 2"

From the assorted cream fat quarters, cut a *total* of:
- 12 squares, 2⅜" × 2⅜"

From the assorted black, gray, and brown fat quarters, cut a *total* of:
- 12 squares, 2⅜" × 2⅜"
- 6 squares, 2" × 2"

From the light gray crossweave fabric, cut:
- 7 strips, 6¾" × 42"
- 6 strips, 5" × 42"; crosscut into 17 strips, 5" × 12½"

From the gray plaid for binding, cut:
- 7 strips, 2½" × 42"

making the half-square-triangle units

Press seam allowances in the directions indicated by the arrows.

IF USING TRIANGLE PAPERS

1. Layer a 10" A square right sides together with a 10" B square, placing the lighter square on top. Place a piece of 2" triangle paper on top of the lighter print.

2. Shorten your stitch to half the normal length. Stitch on all the dashed lines. Cut apart on the solid lines using a rotary cutter and ruler.

3. With the paper still in place, press the seam allowances toward the darker triangles. Remove the paper by pulling on it from the middle, near the seam. Clip the dog-ears to make 16 half-square-triangle units measuring 2½" square, including seam allowances.

4. Repeat steps 1–3 using the remaining A and B squares to make a total of 12 sets of 16 matching units. (That's 192 units total, if you're counting!)

IF NOT USING TRIANGLE PAPERS

1. Draw a diagonal line from corner to corner on the wrong side of the lighter A or B 2⅞" squares.

2. Layer a marked square on a darker A or B 2⅞" square, right sides together. Sew ¼" from both sides of the drawn line. Cut the unit apart on the marked line to make two half-square-triangle units measuring 2½" square, including seam allowances. Repeat to make a total of 12 sets of 16 matching units.

Make 12 sets of 16 matching units, 2½" × 2½".

FINISHED QUILT:
58" × 74½"
FINISHED BLOCK:
12" × 12"

70 ♥ snuggle up!

making the blocks

The instructions below are for making one block. Repeat to make a total of 12 blocks.

1 Center and sew C triangles to opposite sides of a D square. Trim the dog-ears even with the square. Center and sew C triangles to the remaining sides of the square. Trim the unit to 6⅛" square, including seam allowances.

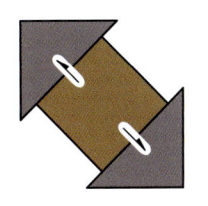

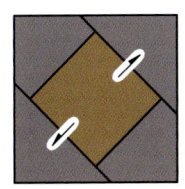

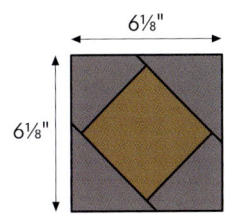

Make 1 unit.

2 Center and sew B triangles to opposite sides of the unit from step 1. Trim the dog-ears even with the unit. Center and sew B triangles to the remaining sides of the unit. Trim the center unit to 8½" square, including seam allowances.

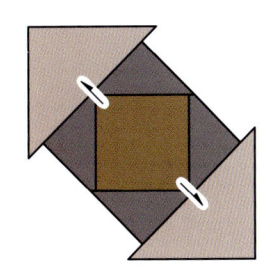

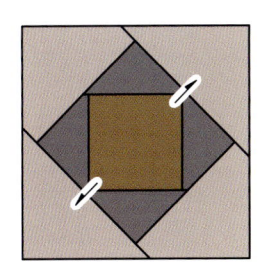

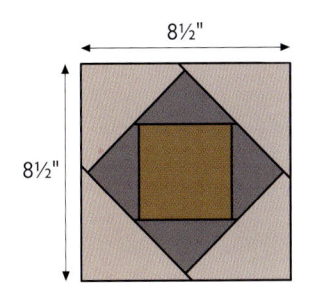

Make 1 center unit.

getting cozy with Lisa Bongean

If there's a chill in the air, I'm sure to have chicken soup on the stove. Booyah!

When I'm ready to snuggle up with a quilt, I also need a grandbaby or two.

If I were the chancellor of Cozy College, my school uniform would be plaid flannel.

Batting is the unseen hero in making a quilt cozy. Here's my choice for a quilt you can wrap up with: Luna.

If there's a bowl of popcorn and my favorite beverage, I'm having homemade caramel corn and water with lemon, please.

When I'm curled under a quilt, the fabric backing is often just as visible to me as the top. So here's my tip for choosing backing fabric: Use the same fabric line, and place extra blocks in the backing.

For me, a quilt to curl up with has to at least be washed many times.

My happy place to snuggle up with a quilt is on my outdoor living porch with the fireplace turned on.

Color has a vibe for many people. Other than the color combination I used in this book, a color combination that says "cozy" to me is scrappy, using all the colors!

LisaBongean.com

rustic retreat

3 Using units that match the B fabric in step 2, join four matching half-square-triangle units, noting the orientation of the units. Make four side units measuring 2½" × 8½".

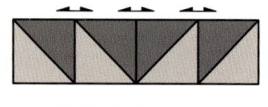

Make 4 side units,
2½" × 8½".

4 Lay out four 2½" A squares, four side units, and one center unit from step 2 in three rows. The A fabric should be the same throughout. Sew the squares and units into rows. Join the rows to make a block measuring 12½" square, including seam allowances. Repeat the steps to make a total of 12 blocks.

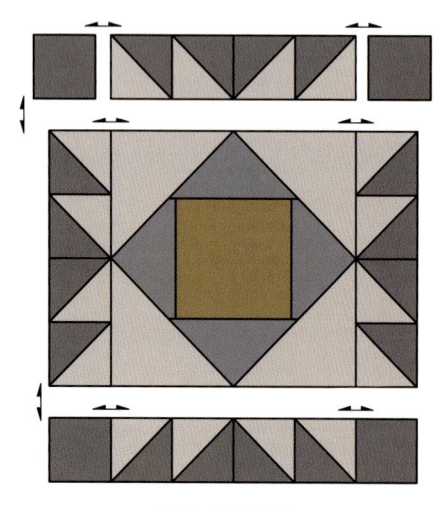

Make 12 blocks,
12½" × 12½".

assembling the quilt top

1 Draw a diagonal line from corner to corner on the wrong side of the cream 2⅜" squares. Layer a marked square on a black, gray, or brown 2⅜" square, right sides together. Sew ¼" from both sides of the drawn line. Cut the unit apart on the marked line to make two half-square-triangle units measuring 2" square, including seam allowances. Repeat to make 24 units.

Make 24 units,
2" × 2".

2 Lay out four matching cream plaid 2" squares, four half-square-triangle units, and one black, gray, or brown 2" square in three rows. Sew the squares and units into rows. Join the rows to make a star unit measuring 5" square, including seam allowances. Make six units.

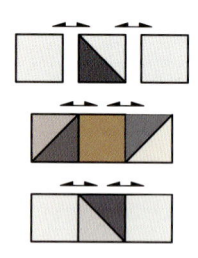

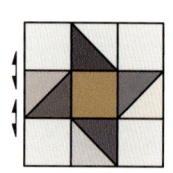

Make 6 star units,
5" × 5".

3 Join three blocks and two light gray 5" × 12½" strips to make a block row measuring 12½" × 45½", including seam allowances. Make four rows.

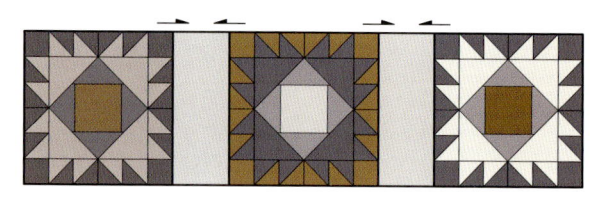

Make 4 block rows,
12½" × 45½".

4 Join three light gray 5" × 12½" strips and two star units to make a sashing row measuring 5" × 45½", including seam allowances. Make three rows.

Make 3 sashing rows,
5" × 45½".

5 Join the block rows and sashing rows, alternating the positions as shown in the quilt assembly diagram on page 73. The quilt top should measure 45½" × 62", including seam allowances.

72 ♥ snuggle up!

6 Join the light gray 6¾"-wide strips end to end. From the pieced strip, cut two 62"-long strips and two 58"-long strips. Sew the longer strips to the left and right sides of the quilt top. Sew the shorter strips to the top and bottom edges. The quilt top should measure 58" × 74½".

finishing the quilt

For more details on any finishing steps, visit ShopMartingale.com/HowtoQuilt for free downloadable information.

1 Layer the quilt top with batting and backing; baste the layers together.

2 Quilt by hand or machine. Lisa's quilt is machine quilted with an allover design of spiral boxes.

3 Use the gray plaid 2½"-wide strips to make binding and then attach the binding to the quilt.

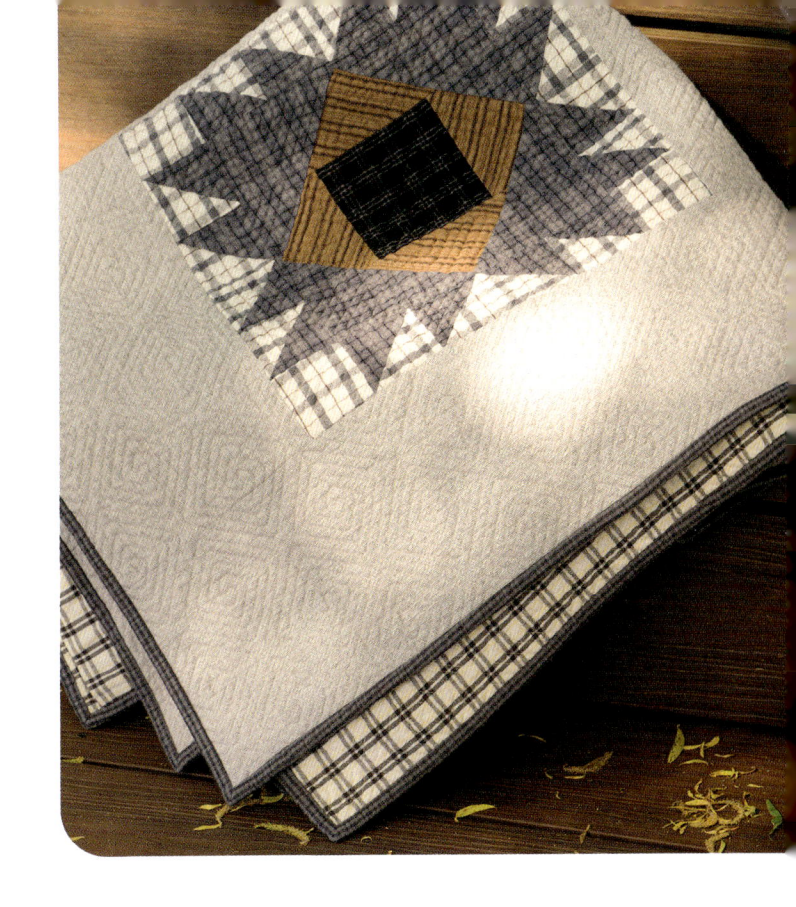

Quilt assembly

rustic retreat ♥ 73

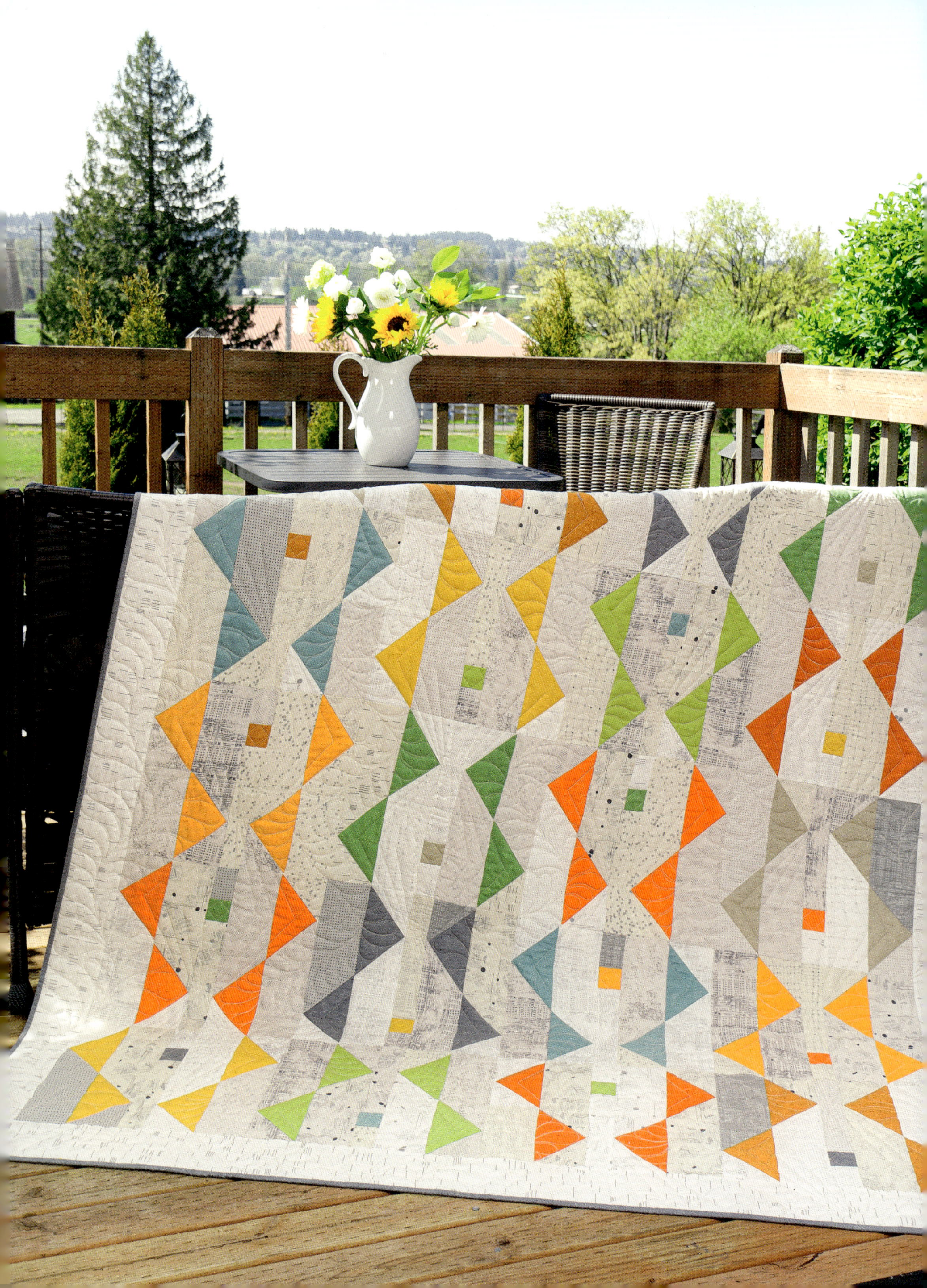

paper planes

Using the common folded-corner technique to turn two squares and a rectangle into three triangles (á la flying geese), Brigitte Heitland presents a quilt that's unique and also easier than it looks. Pretty much like folding a rectangle to make a paper airplane, you can fold one fabric rectangle into something that soars!

Designed by Brigitte Heitland; pieced by Alison Dale; quilted by Crystal Zagnoli of the Quilted Cricket

materials

Yardage is based on 42"-wide fabric. Fat quarters measure 18" × 21". Brigitte used Spotted and Modern Backgrounds: Even More Paper, both by Zen Chic for Moda Fabrics.

3⅞ yards *total* of assorted light prints for blocks

10 fat quarters of assorted dark prints for blocks

¾ yard of light print for border

⅝ yard of gray print for binding

3¾ yards of fabric for backing

67" × 73" piece of batting

cutting

All measurements include ¼" seam allowances.

From the assorted light prints, cut a *total* of:
- 80 pieces, 3½" × 6½"
- 160 squares, 3½" × 3½"
- 20 strips, 2" × 8¾"
- 20 pieces, 2" × 2¾"

From *each* of the assorted dark prints, cut:
- 8 pieces, 3½" × 6½" (80 total)
- 2 squares, 2" × 2" (20 total)

From the light print for border, cut:
- 7 strips, 3½" × 42"

From the gray print, cut:
- 7 strips, 2½" × 42"

FINISHED QUILT:
60½" × 66½"
FINISHED BLOCK:
13½" × 12"

76 ♥ snuggle up!

making the blocks

Press seam allowances in the directions indicated by the arrows.

1. Draw a diagonal line from corner to corner on the wrong side of the light 3½" squares. Place a marked square on one end of a dark piece, right sides together. Sew on the marked line. Trim the excess corner fabric ¼" from the stitched line. Place a marked square on the opposite end of the dark piece. Sew and trim as before to make a flying-geese unit measuring 3½" × 6½", including seam allowances. Make 80 units.

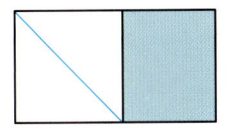

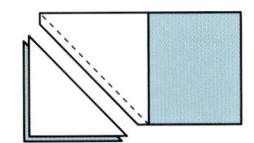

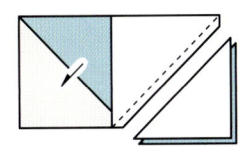

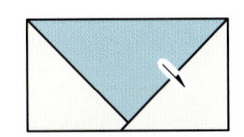

Make 80 units, 3½" × 6½".

2. Join a flying-geese unit and a light 3½" × 6½" piece to make a unit measuring 6½" square, including seam allowances. Make 80 units.

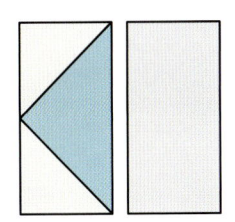

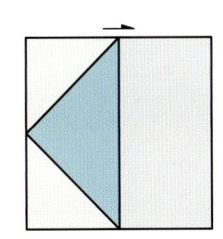

Make 80 units, 6½" × 6½".

getting cozy with Brigitte Heitland

If there's a chill in the air, I'm sure to have a tasty casserole in the oven.

When I'm ready to snuggle up with a quilt, I also need a hot cup of caffe latte.

If I were the chancellor of Cozy College, my school uniform would be allowing everyone to choose their own wardrobe.

Batting is the unseen hero in making a quilt cozy. Here's my choice for a quilt you can wrap up with: bamboo.

If there's a bowl of popcorn and my favorite beverage, I'm having just a simple sweet version like caramel corn with a glass of apple cider.

When I'm curled under a quilt, the fabric backing is often just as visible to me as the top. So here's my tip for choosing backing fabric: play with the leftovers from the quilt top.

For me, a quilt to curl up with has to at least be 60" square.

My happy place to snuggle up with a quilt is my hammock.

Color has a vibe for many people. Other than the color combination I used in this book, a color combination that says "cozy" to me is naturals with black, mustard, and rust.

BrigitteHeitland.de

paper planes

3 Lay out four units from step 2, one light 2" × 2¾" piece, one dark square, and one light 2" × 8¾" strip, rotating the bottom units as shown. The dark print should be the same in all of the flying-geese units. Sew the pieces into columns. Join the columns to make a block measuring 14" × 12½". Make 20 blocks.

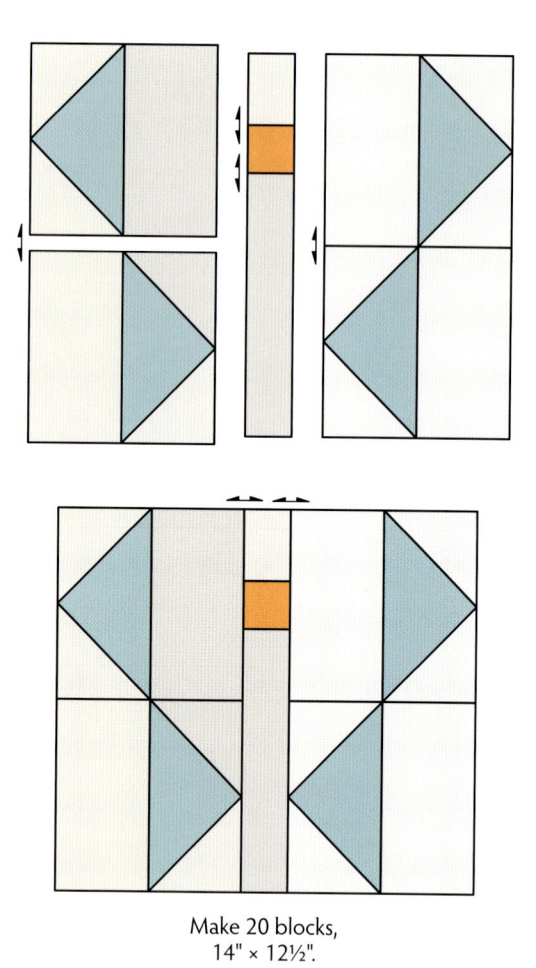

Make 20 blocks, 14" × 12½".

PLAN AHEAD

Before assembling the blocks one at a time in step 3, you may want to pair the small dark squares with sets of four matching flying-geese units. That way you'll be sure you like all the color pairings before you get to the last couple of blocks and don't like your choices!